Say It Out Loud

Say It Out Loud

Journey of a Real Cowboy

Adam Sutton and Neil McMahon

RANDOM HOUSE AUSTRALIA

Random House Australia Pty Ltd
100 Pacific Highway, North Sydney NSW 2060
www.randomhouse.com.au

Sydney New York Toronto
London Auckland Johannesburg

First published by Random House Australia, 2007

National Library of Australia
Cataloguing-in-Publication Entry

Sutton, Adam, 1974–.
Say it out loud.

ISBN 978 1 74166 545 1.

1. Sutton, Adam, 1974–. 2. Horsemen and horsewomen – Australia – Biography. 3. Rodeo performers – Australia – Biography. 4. Ex-convicts – Australia – Biography. 5. Gay men – Australia – Biography. 6. Actors – Australia – Biography. I. McMahon, Neil. II. Title.

798.2092

Cover photograph by Steven Siewert, courtesy of Fairfax Photolibrary
Cover design by saso content & design pty ltd
Sketch on pii by Brooke Stevens aged 16
Typeset in 12/18 pt Berling Roman by Post Pre-press Group, Brisbane, Queensland
Printed and bound by Griffin Press, South Australia
10 9 8 7 6 5 4 3 2 1

For our parents

Author's note

AS A writer, it's a challenge to help anyone transfer their life from their mind and their memory to the page, but it's even more difficult when the subject is a dear friend and you have been involved in some of the events described. It becomes an emotional as well as a professional test.

I met Adam in 2003, on his first visit to a gay night-club in Sydney. I had never met anyone like him. He was, as you will often find him to be in these pages, a boisterous, rowdy, fun-loving larrikin from the first moment. Within minutes of our meeting, he'd shown me just how fun-loving he could be. I tried to strike up a conversation, but he was too busy dancing. Then, without warning, he picked me up, put one arm under my knees, the other under my back, spun me around and threw me. I landed on my arse a metre or so away. I'm a giant six foot five in the old scale, just shy of 200 centimetres, and I can safely say that no one had ever done that to me before. We have been mates ever since.

Now leap forward three years, to Adam's decision to tell his story publicly. He first did so in the *Sydney Morning Herald*, where I work as a journalist. I'd long known that Adam had a remarkable story to tell. The release of *Brokeback Mountain* – the gay cowboy movie – gave us the opportunity to tell it. We did so in March 2006; then we both took part in an ABC program on Adam's life; then came this book. But although I've been a significant part of Adam's story, I don't appear anywhere in the main narrative of this book. It was simply too jarring to have the writer who helped him put his story to paper also be a figure in the story we were telling.

Does that mean we have had to leave out anything important? No, we haven't. This is Adam's story. It's his life. I've helped him with the words, but the courage and honesty you will discover here are all his, told from his perspective.

There are others whose presence here needs some explanation. On occasion, we have changed the names of people and sometimes omitted or obscured details of time and place to protect their privacy. We have always tried to do so without compromising the integrity of the story being told.

Most importantly, this book includes significant detail concerning Adam Gosden, a young man who died in an accident for which Adam Sutton was to blame. After Adam made his decision to tell his story, he decided to contact the Gosden family. He wanted to minimise any distress they would experience from hearing him describe those events publicly, and also to invite them to provide a fuller picture of the man they had lost so that we would be able to treat his memory with due respect.

The Gosdens handled this approach with immense courage and honesty, but understandably chose not to be involved in this book. Adam's contact with the family was largely made possible through the Gosdens' priest, Father Reg Callinan, of the Morisset parish. Father Callinan, who knew Adam Gosden, provided us with the biographical detail included in Chapter 5. I would also like to acknowledge his gentle and generous involvement in what was a difficult circumstance for both Adam and the Gosden family and particularly his simple, honest and heartfelt counsel as he helped us understand the true meaning of forgiveness and reconciliation. Father Callinan has a unique place in this story, as the only person to have looked each of these young men in the eye and recognised the goodness in both of them.

Little has been easy about the process of bringing Adam's story to the world, but I'm proud to have been able to help him achieve what he set out to do: say it out loud.

Neil McMahon

Prologue

WE KNOW all about death, Dad and I.

I am in the dock at Newcastle Supreme Court; he is in the witness box. A man is dead, and I am to blame. Dad is doing his best to make sure they don't lock me away, telling the judge that he knows what it's like for a man to live with death on his conscience – he fought, and killed, in Vietnam.

He will live with what he's done for the rest of his days. And that is punishment enough.

The dead man was an Adam, too. I talk to him sometimes and tell him I wish I had died that day, not him. I wonder what Adam Gosden would have become if he had lived and I had died instead. What if we had never encountered each other at all? No one knows how it haunts me.

I sit in court thinking that though all these people can see me and they all know what I've done, they don't *know me*, the core of me, and nothing the judge says can change who I am or what I feel at this moment, waiting for the verdict. At my core is hatred, all reserved for myself, and it eats at me and cannot come out in words.

No one knows how good I am at hiding my secrets. Some secrets are worth keeping. Some are shameful. Others you don't understand at all, and you keep them secret because to say them out loud would suggest you know what they mean. I have secrets like that, and I wonder when I'll understand them. Maybe never.

I wait for the verdict, and I tell myself I have to keep it all in. If I let it out, if I allow myself to feel, it will stop me in my tracks, and I refuse to surrender this moment to tears.

The judge begins to speak. His burden – deciding what he should do with my life – will soon become mine.

What will I do with it, once he's handed it back to me?

Chapter 1

I WAS only 19 then and, looking back, I wonder what the judge must have thought as he sat there looking at me, deciding what to do. I appeared younger than my years – blond-haired, fresh-faced, fit, tanned. On another day at another time he might have seen bright eyes and an easy smile. It's there in photos of the time, before I went from being a normal teenager to a defendant. And it's there in other photos, too – of my dad. At 19, he looked like that: a healthy and strapping young man with everything in front of him.

My father came to Australia as a ten-quid migrant in 1958. Britain was not long free of the shadow of World War II, which had ended in the year he was born, and to his parents Australia seemed peaceful, rich, hot and far away – almost like another planet.

They were met by relatives waiting for them in Western Australia, and at 13 Dad quickly adapted to the alien life. His accent disappeared. He discovered his skin could go brown. He learned how to handle a wave, and later a surfboard. But it was in the east that the money, people and jobs were, and it was not long before they moved to Sydney.

My mother, Barbara O'Brien, was born and bred in Sydney. She had three brothers, a mother with the patience of a saint, and a father who'd seen action in the war. Perhaps Lenny O'Brien had seen too much; he sometimes seemed to resent the world, and turned to drink. But my mum was loyal, inclined to smile even when it might have seemed easier to frown, and ready to grasp life. She was four years younger than Dad – 15 to his 19 – when they met at Harbord Beach one summer afternoon in 1964. For a while she thought she didn't have a hope: the good-looking bloke with all the mates and the easy manner seemed hard to tame and all the girls wanted him. They became friends before they were anything else and ran with the same crowd, going to parties and picnics, and spending days at the beach. But they both knew there was something more between them. The attachment and attraction grew and soon they became a couple, with eyes only for each other. It was a different time; people were younger when they settled down, and Mum and Dad were already considering a future together. What they hadn't counted on was conscription.

It wasn't a war then, at least not as most people thought of war. Dad and his mates were told it was a police action – keeping law and order, maintaining the peace. It seemed an adventure and an opportunity, so he didn't object. No one imagined what it would become. Dad spent a year in training, first in New South Wales, then south at Puckapunyal in Victoria. By 1966 he was on a plane on his way to Vietnam, a member of 5 RAR battalion. My mum was only 16 and promised to wait for him. They thought it would be for a year. Dad had just turned 21.

Dad landed in Saigon, then moved to the coast and set up camp beside a beach. They had strict instructions that they weren't allowed to swim, and before long they started to suspect their mission was more serious than they had been led to believe. After a month, they were out on patrol on search-and-destroy missions, and then they knew for certain: it was a war; they weren't just keeping the peace. My dad and his mates patrolled the jungle, looking for the enemy, but the problem was that they were outsiders in a civil war, and often had no idea who the enemy was or what he looked like. Once, Dad's company saw some distant figures walking through a village and fired on them. Later, they discovered they'd killed a father and his child, not enemy combatants. So many rounds had been fired no one knew who was responsible for the fatal shots, but all the Australians were free to imagine that they were to blame.

Mum wrote to my father every day. Dad would get the letters in a bundle and devour them as soon as he received them. But gradually it got harder to read of life back home, and he'd wait and read them over a few days. Mum told him she was waiting and would still be waiting when he came home. Dad would tell her: *Get on with your life, it's too uncertain, I might not come home*. But she was not about to give up.

Ten months into his year of service, Dad was given leave. Sometimes they were allowed to spend a few days in Hong Kong on R&R, other times they were given a break from daily duty but stayed in Vietnam. They needed it – relief from the daily grind and stress of the war, time to relax and let their hair down. One night Dad and a mate were out on the tiles in Vietnam, doing just that. They had too much to drink. Full as boots, they decided on a lark to break the 10 pm curfew and gatecrash the American officers' club, which was off limits to soldiers like them. Fuelled by booze and bravado, they got into a scuffle with a guard and threw him into the river that ran under the bridge leading to the club. After that, Dad was set upon by a bunch of American officers and beaten to a pulp. He was saved only because an Australian officer was also drinking at the club that night and recognised him, but not before they'd fractured his skull, ruptured his eardrum and left him with a clot on the brain that paralysed him temporarily down his left side.

Dad spent two weeks in a local hospital, and was still there on the day he was due to return to his battalion from leave. That same day, the men of B Company – Dad's company – went out on patrol and ran over a massive bomb. Seven Australians died that day, and two more died later from their injuries. They were Dad's mates and he knew he should have been with them. He had to go to the morgue to identify two of them, friends whose faces had been burned beyond recognition.

They flew Dad home on a hospital plane. His physical injuries were healing, but the psychological wounds were only starting to emerge. There was no counselling then, no thought given to the damage that had been done to minds as well as bodies.

Mum, only 17, found it difficult to understand his torments; no one could pretend to. She knew he had changed, though: he would squat on his haunches rather than sit on a chair – force of habit – and there were moments when he'd get lost in thought, staring at small things that meant nothing. An open drawer could hold his gaze while his mind wandered to places only he knew about.

But his love for my mother was not in question, and nor was her love for him. They were married on 2 December 1967, and moved into a rented flat together. Mum, blessed with energy and natural joy, wanted them to embrace life and would think of ways to fill their days – water-skiing, horseriding, parties. But at night, she would wake to find him covered in sweat and terrified from a nightmare. He would be dreaming of the jungle.

Mum couldn't do anything. No one could. And Dad didn't want sympathy. He thought seeking understanding was futile, so he said nothing. But his love for her kept him there; without it, he thinks he would surely have run away.

My father wanted to be strong for Mum, and in 1968 she needed all his support when one of her brothers, John, was conscripted. Unlike Dad, he didn't want to go, saw no adventure in it, hated the thought of even holding a gun. He was in Vietnam only three weeks before he was killed in battle. Mum was eight weeks pregnant, but miscarried after she heard the news. The shock and grief claimed her unborn baby. Her brother was given a military funeral.

Mum and Dad built a happy marriage in spite of it all. Dad learned to hide everything that saddened him. Booze helped bury it sometimes. But my mum was his rock. They both worked two jobs to save money to travel around Britain and Europe for a couple of years. It was the absence and adventure they needed, although they knew they were never going to stay. In late 1973, they returned to Australia, planning to settle in Western Australia, but changed their minds. It felt too far away, so they drove back to Sydney, across the Nullarbor.

It was my first trip across that desert plain, because Mum was pregnant. I arrived on 21 October 1974 – week 40 of her pregnancy, not late but pushing it – and I was big: nearly four-and-a-half kilos. Mum thought I was never coming, and that set my habit of a lifetime: arriving when I pleased, always a handful.

My first home was a flat on the northern beaches, then Mum and Dad moved to a house in Lane Cove. That's where I learned to walk, then to run. Once on my feet, I never stopped moving.

Chapter 2

THERE WERE holes in the roof of our house in Mowbray Road, but if you'd been able to sit up there and look down at the lives inside, you'd have seen that the holes didn't matter to us.

My sister Sally arrived in 1977, two weeks before my third birthday, and Leah joined us a few years later. From the beginning I adored my little sisters. In my memory, our family was a union of noise and joy. We had dogs and birds and cats, pots and pans to catch the rain when it came through the roof, neighbours who sometimes wondered about the mad family next door, and dinner at the table every night. We were neither poor nor rich, but never wanted for anything that mattered. In any case, everything that mattered to me was outside, and fresh air cost nothing.

If we lacked for anything, I only noticed it when I'd go to other people's houses and see how they lived, what they had and the rules they lived by. *Get out, take your shoes off, you can't do that, you can't eat this*. As I saw it, there seemed to be less *stuff* in our house, and fewer rules, but more love and more fun.

At our place, anyone was welcome – *In the front door you come.* Dad had his own scaffolding business then. He worked hard, played rugby league at a local club and drank with his mates. Mum was a hairdresser and usually worked from home. She fed us, drove us where we needed to be, tried to stop us worrying the neighbours, and drew up the daily roster that kept the house running – wash the dishes, dry the dishes, put the dishes away, feed the dogs and birds. We shared the chores as we got older, and sometimes tried to dodge them. But ours was not a home of strict demands or raised voices. Mum: busy, happy, smiling, laughing – those are the memories of her that stick. And I worshipped Dad; I was too young then to see the ghosts that haunted him.

I spent nearly every day outdoors, running wild, or as wild as the quiet streets of the northern suburbs of Sydney allowed. It was clear early on that I belonged in the bush, but for the time being Lane Cove would have to do.

If I was going to be stuck in the boring suburbs of a big city, this was as good a place as any. We lived on two acres in a rundown old cottage that had once been the Lane Cove dairy. Mr Nissen rented it to Mum and Dad for $25 a week on the condition he could keep using the yard to tinker with his vintage cars. The yard was full of them.

To me, those two acres were like a world of their own – there was space to run and climb and ride and hide. The yard was so big we had eight neighbours – on either side of us, opposite, and in the laneway that ran along the rear of our home. None of them adored me. Not Mrs Davis: I'd climb her trees, hit her flowers with a stick, and steal fruit from her trees, driving her more than once to cross the street for discussions with my mother about the wayward nature of her boy. Not Mr Honeyman: he was exotic – Hawaiian, I think – and his dogs could be incited to chase me and my mates up the street and down the lane. And not the Lebanese man who ran the general business on the corner, whose son Ali went to the same school as me. At the age of 10, I asked him for a job at a salary of 20 cents an hour, or he could pay me in Paddle Pops, whichever he was willing to part with. He refused, and by way of revenge I set up my own business on the footpath right outside his shop with a friend from next door – gathering toys we no longer wanted, wrapping them in paper and offering a lucky dip at 50 cents a go to his customers as they went in and out.

At the very back of our yard there was a huge bush where I'd meet with my mates and hatch plots in peace. Our initials were carved in the trunk, listing the members by name – Jason Smith, captain; Adam Sutton, vice-captain; then those of lesser rank: Scott Johnston, Gary Swan and others. Jason and I would give orders and the gang would carry out the operation – a standard mission being, say, to run to the service station at the top of the street to nick a packet of chewie. We considered that a triumph. Other times we would divide into teams and fight wars amongst ourselves. We were the coolest. Other kids – the dags, the nerds, the teachers' pets, anyone who didn't fit in – were there to be mocked when the mood took us. We could gossip, ostracise and punish – cruel as only kids can be. We ruled our own world, or thought we did. Everywhere you turned there were adults who appeared to believe they were in charge – parents, teachers, neighbours, uncles, aunts, grandparents – but they were at worst a nuisance and an occasional interruption to our mastery of our universe.

But it could backfire. We were never as cool or as smart as we imagined ourselves to be. I remember one poor kid who was widely rumoured to have been caught sticking his finger up a chicken's bum. It was a story that unfairly earned him the nickname Chicken Fucker and a reputation as a legitimate target for our nastiest instincts. I could be as brutal as the rest, but I would eventually get my just deserts. Once, when he was in the toilets at school, I yelled to my fellow gang members, *Come on, let's go in and give him a head job*, a phrase I had heard somewhere and which I thought described giving someone a good wallop about the head. Others knew better. That incident temporarily blackened my good name, but I survived, and learned to watch what I said and who I said it to, especially when I had no idea what I was saying.

I'd have been better off also learning not to be so cruel – I'd eventually be as familiar as David Greenwood with the struggles of feeling like I didn't fit in, and of fearing the taunts and contempt of my mates.

If I was cool but sometimes clueless in the playground, the same held true in the classroom. In my seven years at Mowbray Public School, the best report I ever got was in my first year, when I was judged adequate on the three-point scale they used to assess six-year-olds. You got a plus sign for Above Average, a tick for Average and a minus for Below Average. My report was a sea of ticks. But by the end of 1983, things were on the slide. *Adam's concentration needs to be improved,* Miss Mathieson reported, accurately echoing the contents of every school report I received from that day on. A year later, when I was 10, I was *making little or no effort,* and was *hampered by an apparent lack of motivation.*

I was never going to be a classroom star, but if it bothered me I can't remember it now, because for all my failings as a pupil there was never a doubt that I loved school. It was just that I loved it more for what went on outside the classroom than anything that went on in it. I made little effort at my desk, but threw everything into life when I escaped it.

That same year, 1984, I got my first girlfriend, Aleisha, a small thrill because by then girlfriends were something we vaguely believed we had to have. They were a status symbol and a minimal inconvenience. All you had to do was hold hands in the playground, have an occasional kiss in the toilets and show up at important social occasions.

I kept my end of the bargain and Aleisha kept hers, coming to my 10th birthday party that year. But she didn't interfere with my main reason for living, which continued to be having adventures with my mates. Gary Swan and I once combined the two: adventure and the search for true love. *This weekend,* I told him, *me and you are going to go find a girlfriend each,* as if we were on the lookout for a lizard or a dog.

Where do you reckon we could go look?

Well, let's start down the park and if we find no one there we'll go to the next park. We'll just cruise around on our bikes and find one.

It was a mission, I see now, more about the journey than the destination.

DAD HAD a small boat – a half-cabin runabout – and loved fishing. He handed the love down, taking me out on the water as a tyke. I had a rod in my hand when I was three. The water was Sydney Harbour, with its big bridge and its mansions and its Opera House. The harbour was so big and the boat so small that it was scary at times out in the swell, rattling towards the Heads. But it also convinced me that if Dad could do this he could surely do anything. My love and trust was sealed out there on the water, and didn't waver even when things went wrong.

On one trip my father warned me over and over not to touch the fish he'd just caught. I touched it anyway and cut my finger, leaving me sobbing and bleeding as we headed back to shore, and temporarily banned from future expeditions once we got there. I cried and cried. I wanted to be with him, casting a line.

I loved fishing enough that I wrote about it, something I did often as a kid. I've kept them all – piles of drawings and stories, painstakingly composed and illustrated using every colour in the Texta packet. I have one small book held together with masking tape: *Fishing With Dad, by Adam*. And reading it now reminds me of how much I loved those days on the water.

We went on a fishing trip. First we went to Fort Denison. Then I went to the toilet. When I got off the toilet I went back to my fishing line and I felt a big tug. It was a very big fish. It was a big trevally. Then we reached the wharf. I went up the stairs and I was just in time for the weighing of the fish. Then I heard Daddy yell and it was because we had won the fishing contest.

I illustrated our victory with sketches of Dad and me – two stick figures – casting our lines into a sea of blue Texta. The larger one – my dad – had two dots for eyes, a big smile and no nose. I'm shouting and waving in triumph.

Dad's mother, Nan, lived in McMahons Point, a hop and a

skip from the harbour shore, and when I was old enough they'd let me sit down there all day on my own with my rod, catching what I could. I loved going to Nan's – a weekend there offered its own freedoms, adventures and dangers. The main peril often was Nan herself. It occasionally seemed a wonder to her that we were members of the same species, let alone the same family. I tested her patience at every turn, even when I wasn't awake.

For a time Nan let me share her big bed, until the night she woke to find me in the middle of a bad dream and hitting her across the head in my sleep, ending that night-time arrangement for good. Throughout the day she tried in vain to keep order, even keeping a rolled-up newspaper at hand. She never had any intention of using it, but must have believed it carried more weight than words. *You do that one more time, Adam Sutton, and I'll hit you with this.* She never did, though, not even when, at nine, I broke a branch off the umbrella tree in her yard and advised her that if she hit me with that, I would hit her with *this*.

But the phone was Nan's most effective weapon, especially when my manners or mischief defeated her. She was old school. Manners mattered. So if, for instance, her neighbour Mrs Loxley was coming for afternoon tea, she was to be addressed by me as Mrs Loxley and not by her first name, which I knew to be Win. *You be on your best behaviour when she gets here,* Nan would say, and when Mrs Loxley arrived I would cheerfully greet her at the door.

Hello, Win.

It's not Win, Nan would scold. *It's Mrs Loxley.*

Then I'd prop on the couch, eating a bowl of ice-cream as gruesomely as I could manage, dribbling it everywhere just to get a rise. Win would announce, *Harriet, I'm leaving,* and Nan would rouse at me, then reach for the phone to call Mum.

Barbara, come and get him. I will not have him in this house.

Mum was always coming to get me. But Nan would give in and take me back for visits, and our war was more an affectionate battle of wills than one of outright hostility. I was a mischievous boy rather than a bad one. And besides, I was not the only member of the family she found an occasional trial.

No one found Pop – Mum's father – easy to deal with, and Nan found him particularly difficult. *I will not sit down to Christmas dinner with him,* she announced one year. She regarded him as surly and uncouth, and it was not hard to see what she was on about. Pop seemed a bit of a handful even to me. He drank, perhaps too much, and after the death of his wife, who I can barely remember, he drank more. Nan did come to Christmas dinner that year and endured Pop tapping his fork on his plate while she said grace. They were never destined to bond.

Pop lived in a small house in Crows Nest. He'd sit at a table, on top of which, in my memory, were piles of copper coins stacked in 10-cent piles and a bowl of sugar. He'd sit in near darkness, and the legs of the table sat in saucers of water. This, he explained to me, was so the ants would drown before they could climb the table legs and get to his bowl of sugar. It made sense to me. Actually, it seemed incredibly clever. But Pop was a loner, not much used to anyone, certainly not young kids like me. I think I was more of a mystery to him than I was even to Nan, and he was a mystery to everyone else. War had left its silent scars everywhere in our family.

I WAS two when I first sat on a horse, just for show, and on my fifth birthday I rode one. His name was Charlie, and Mum and Dad had organised him as a treat for my birthday party. It was the moment that would eventually come to matter the most, but I can only imagine it rather than remember it. Soon, horseriding became a hobby for our whole family. Mum and Dad could both ride, and we three kids learned keenly and fast. We'd hire horses and go on family rides in Ku-ring-gai Chase National Park on weekends. Eventually we got our own horses, the first of which was Buddy – a two-year-old, barely broken in – who we learned to ride quickly because with Buddy it was either that or die trying. He didn't have much of an idea what he was doing, and we had even less. He'd rear and buck, throw and bite, but horses never held any fear for me, even when I was small.

By the time I was 12, the love was running deep. That

year, 1986, I won the Melbourne Cup, as related in a four-page story I wrote that detailed how I trained and rode a horse called Luckyness to victory.

> *On your marks, get set, go. Racing now, Slang in the lead, Jerk is coming second, Aggro coming third, Drongo is coming fourth, Luckyness is coming fifth. Luckyness coming up on the inside, passing Drongo, passing Aggro, passing Jerk and battling it out with Slang. One hundred yards to go and Luckyness pulls away and takes the money. I did it. No, sorry, we did it, didn't we Luckyness. Neigh, neigh, neigh. Well, we got a nice house and lived happily ever after.*

MY SKILL at fishing and riding – and my enthusiasm for writing it all down – suggest I could apply my mind to the things that engaged it, but my school reports show I could just as easily switch it off for long periods. At the end of 1986 my Year 6 teacher packed me off to high school with a warning that if I didn't knuckle down and concentrate, *life will be very frustrating*. She found me lacking in tidiness, obedience, writing, spelling, mathematics, social studies and general behaviour in the library. It didn't seem to matter that I could catch fish or ride horses. But she was right, of course. High school loomed, and things weren't about to get any better.

Chapter 3

I CAN'T remember exactly when I started becoming an apprentice juvenile delinquent, but that's what I became, and I say that with neither pride nor regret. It was just what happened.

In the early days of Year 7, I turned up to school every day, even if I was doing my best not to learn much while I was there. But towards the end of the year, I learned how to wag. I was now under the spell of Willy Barker, who was also in Year 7 but who had the cachet of being the brother of an older Chatswood High student. There were several ways of getting out of a day's school. I'd forge notes from Mum, usually by convincing one of the older girls to copy her signature. At other times we'd get the students in charge of morning roll-call to mark us present, or we'd just turn up for morning assembly, announce our attendance, then disappear for the rest of the day. It would have been bad enough if we'd just left it at that, but we weren't skipping school so we could stay home and watch Ray Martin on *The Midday Show*, or kick a footy around the park. We weren't even going to the movies. We were stealing paint and graffitiing trains. We could happily ride the trains all day.

A teenage graffiti artist – and I became one around the time of my 13th birthday that October – may look like a destructive punk motivated by the urge to vandalise and destroy. But there was more to it than that. For starters, you belonged to something, and I belonged to the graffiti group more easily and comfortably than I could ever fit into French or music class. Graffiti artists were known as bombers, and graffiti gangs were known as crews, and there were a lot of bombers and crews working the railroads and underpasses of Sydney back then. You knew them by their signatures – PiC was Partners in Crime, LSD was Leave Sydney Devastated, US stood for Under Suspicion. Within a crew, each member had his own signature (mine was *Usual*) and you became a crew member by invitation only. It was not offered lightly.

I was there for the thrill of putting myself on what seemed to be the very edge of civilised behaviour – it was the adrenaline surge, coming at warp speed – but others saw themselves as renegade artists of real talent. Public vandalism was only part of the picture; most of them didn't even see it as that. Public art, a political statement, whatever they called it, it was not ugly to them. As a sign of their seriousness the artists invited you to join a crew only if they liked your pieces, as we called them – the same word you'd use for any other work of art. The Chatswood High boys became part of the Under Suspicion crew, but we hankered to be a part of the bigger, more respected PiC. It was not much of an ambition for a young teenager to have, but it was something – I wanted to be a Partner in Crime. Artist or criminal? In truth, I was both of those things, and a few others, too, among them, a thief, because I needed paint to complete the piece or commit the crime. None of us had much money, so we had to nick it. I was also a teenage shoplifter, and I'm not going to tell you there was anything artistic about that.

As 1987 turned into 1988 – the year of Australia's Bicentenary, marking 200 years since Sydney officially became a penal colony – I was doing my best to behave like a petty criminal. I was a convict in the making, the only difference being that I never got nabbed. We came close several times, but fleeing the railway guards who caught us in the act only added to the thrill. It might have been less of an adrenaline charge if they'd ever managed to catch us and we'd had to face the consequences, but as long as they didn't I was happy to experience the rush. And there were times when it was truly satisfying, even when we weren't in danger of being taken into custody. Under the Hampton Road bridge in Artarmon, you could spend an entire day composing a piece without any interruption at all.

Eventually, wagging became as much the norm as

spending a whole day at school. Skipping two or three days a week was not unusual, and it says a lot for how skilled we were at doing it, or how bad the teachers were at keeping track of us, that we hardly ever had to explain ourselves. They were stupid and dangerous days, which I can't defend, but I'm also not going to say I didn't enjoy it, or that I wasn't learning something – I was independent, street-smart, enterprising and I knew everything there was to know about mixing and blending paint, none of which was on the New South Wales high school curriculum. I was also on the verge of becoming caught up in a world I'd never escape – it wouldn't have been too big a leap from nicking a cheap tin of paint to nicking a car, and it would have been all downhill from there.

But my addiction was to thrills, wherever they came from, and I could also get them in other places – places where there were no laws to break. I had another life away from the wagging and the crews and the paint and the stealing.

I CAN only put my affinity for high school gymnastics down to the fact that I thrived on disaster being only a moment away. While the other teachers were sending home reports using words like *inattentive*, *restless* and *talkative*, Ms Vaughan the PE teacher was hailing my *excellent record*, my fitness levels, and telling Mum and Dad I was *a talented pupil*. By Year 8, I was becoming an accomplished trampolinist. It may have been that hurling myself upside down through the air – and the associated danger of missing the trampoline and landing on my head – was not too far removed from the crazy things I was getting up to outside school. Both required a certain mindless bravado to pull off, and I had plenty of that. In 1987, I was good enough to take part in the Combined High Schools championships, where I came sixth in the entire state in my age group.

If gymnastics class was one of my other worlds, Ku-ring-gai Chase National Park, where the family still spent many weekends on horseback, was another. I'd become a skilled and fearless rider, and every other thrill paled next to this one: hurtling along a bush track on Buddy. He had become my sole property, mainly because Sally and Leah thought he was a dangerous nut. Leah had the scars to prove her point, as Buddy had once bitten her on the face. In a sense he was a four-legged version of me, which might explain why I loved him. It was the first but not the last time I would learn that horses are often like humans, and that if you take that as your starting point you can understand them as easily as you can size up a person. As with people, it was believing that they were all the same, or should all be the same, that was the problem.

Buddy didn't scare me at all. I understood him, all his quirks and habits and foibles and flaws. It was a matter of rounding off the rough edges where you could, but accepting them where you couldn't. If Buddy had been a 13-year-old boy, I suspect he might have been talked into painting his name on a train, too. He became my mate, the one I spent weekends with and the one who probably saved me from becoming a full-time troublemaker with my two-legged buddies. There were no laws to break on horseback, and no one could tell me what to do in the saddle because I discovered I could do it all myself. In this world, I had total control.

The same could not be said for life at home. I'm not sure that there was a precise moment when I realised Mum and Dad's marriage was struggling, but I recall building a store of enough moments to know that there were problems. Today, happy and thriving in their 40th year of marriage, they can look back and see what went wrong, and blame it on letting selfishness get the better of both of them for a time. And neither knew then how deeply the scars of war were affecting Dad, or how they might be healed.

I didn't know Dad had once been at war, or if I did it barely registered with me then. I had even less idea that he was still fighting it inside himself two decades later, though looking back now he will tell you he barely understood any of it himself. By 1987, he was 20 years removed from Vietnam, a 42-year-old man with his own business, a wife, a 13-year-old son, and beautiful daughters aged 10 and seven. He lived with us, but also lived with his ghosts.

I can't remember exactly when Dad left, but he did, and suddenly he was living in McMahons Point with Nan. Sally, Leah and I stayed in Lane Cove with Mum; the girls too young to understand – me old enough to grasp it, but not as traumatised or frightened as you'd expect. That the split coincided with the height of my truancy and graffiti period might suggest it upset me more than I am willing to admit, but I think all that probably would have happened anyway. I've never needed much encouragement to take the occasional wrong fork in the road. Mum and Dad's separation probably just made things a little worse than they would otherwise have been, if only for the practical reason that with my parents now in separate households it was even harder for them to keep tabs on me.

After Dad left, Mum did her best to explain to me what had gone wrong. I was proud that she trusted me enough to confide in me. Some of it was beyond true understanding for a 13-year-old, but I'm not sure they really understood it either. People rarely do, when they're in the middle of the misery. I sat on the end of her bed that night, listening, and she swore me to secrecy – the girls were too young to understand, she said, and did not need to know. I can't remember her words now, but I know I came away believing that, whatever their troubles, everything would somehow be okay.

I spent a lot of time with Dad in the awkward months of their separation, mostly on weekends, and Dad also spent a lot of time in the pub. One memory stands out: me waiting outside a hotel in North Sydney. When he came out, we didn't go home to Nan's. Instead he took me down to the harbour's edge, and we sat under the bridge, looking out over the water where he'd taught me to fish. But this time, he needed something from me: my understanding. Dad cried and said he was sorry and that he would try to make things right. I had no doubt at the time that he would, because whatever had happened I'd never lost my absolute trust in him and everything he did and said.

Had I been able to understand the truth of what tortured him, I might not have been so optimistic. On top of everything else, his scaffolding business was struggling and eventually folded. It cost him money and his friendship with his business partner. Financially, this was something we could not afford, but in other ways it was a blessing. Before the separation, Mum and Dad had put a deposit on a house on the Central Coast, so even though things were a little tight we did have somewhere else to go. This was the perfect time to move, the catalyst for a fresh start.

I never knew how my parents resolved their differences, but after six months Dad came home to Lane Cove and they started planning a new beginning. At the start of 1989, Mum and Dad, three kids, dogs, cats, birds and furniture piled into a truck and moved north.

We'd been through a lot that year. Not for the last time, we were a stronger family for it.

Chapter 4

COORANBONG, OUR new home, sat at the base of the Watagan Mountains on the western edge of Lake Macquarie, just a couple of hours north of Sydney – not the outback, not even close, but it was rural and quiet and green enough to seem a world away from the big city and the problems we'd left behind. The name was taken from the Aboriginal word Kour-an-bong, roughly translated as *rocky bottom creek*, and the first white people settled there in 1826. We already knew the town, as Mum's brother, his wife and children lived there, and we'd spent many weekends and holidays on their property; so it wasn't new to us, but it was new enough.

When we arrived, the town had just a few thousand residents, and two of them were household names. For almost a century, Cooranbong had been home to a sizeable population of Seventh-Day Adventists, who had established Avondale College there in 1897 and Sanitarium

Health Foods in 1909. Sanitarium was famous for making the nation's favourite breakfast cereal. The church itself was famous for having in its congregation Lindy and Michael Chamberlain. They had been wrongly accused of murdering their baby daughter Azaria at Uluru nine years before in Australia's most celebrated murder case. By then, Lindy had been released from prison and cleared of the crime, and returned to her husband and children – Aidan, Reagan and Kahlia – at Avondale, where Michael had been a pastor. The Australian media had swamped the place for years. In 1988, Cooranbong went global when Meryl Streep played Lindy in a Hollywood movie and was nominated for an Oscar.

These were Cooranbong's two claims to fame in 1989: Lindy Chamberlain and a breakfast cereal. I ate Weet-Bix and would later become friends with Aidan Chamberlain, but Cooranbong meant only one thing to me when we first arrived – a new world to discover and navigate. Although I hadn't wanted to leave the security of home in Lane Cove, school at Chatswood, Nan's place in McMahons Point and my graffiti gang, my reservations disappeared almost as soon as we arrived. It was a new town, a new school, people I didn't know. Our new home – a four-bedroom brick house on seven acres – had enough obvious potential to stop me pining for Sydney straight away. Most importantly, we now had the space to keep horses at home. Buddy moved into the stables in the backyard. There was also room for a small farmyard of animals if we wanted them, and I did.

We moved there in January, close to the start of the new school year, and I was catching the bus to Year 9 at Morisset High almost immediately. I learned then a skill I would have to apply many times in the years ahead: how to adapt to a new environment in a hurry. I made new friends fast. In a scene straight out of *Ginger Meggs,* two other year niners appeared on bikes outside our new house the afternoon of my first day at school. *You're the new kid, aren't ya?* they said.

And that was that. I was in.

I WAS 14 and wise in many of the ways of the world, but still thick as a brick about others. Sex was one of them. I wasn't even sure what puberty was – I had it partly confused with losing your virginity, and wasn't sure if the hair on my balls was enough to mean I'd made it. I recall sex education at school teaching me where the vulva was and how the penis worked, but not being overly useful in explaining how the two bits of information might be practically combined. Not that it would have been a great help anyway, because my mind was wandering in other directions, and even if I went back to school today I still wouldn't learn how to properly navigate those strange roads.

That year, I shot my load for the first time. I was asleep when it happened, but woke up to the mess and the memory of the pleasure of it. Like all young men, I was amazed: you mean it can pee *and* do that? But then there was the horror that went with it. When it happened, I'd been dreaming about a kid I'd been to school with in Sydney, a boy. I knew almost nothing about sex, but I knew enough to know that this wasn't the way it was supposed to be.

I didn't even know what gay was. The modern put-down – *that's so gay* – had not yet entered the teenage language, but the old Australian favourite *poofter* was an all-purpose playground insult reserved for the most contemptible boys. It was so common and used on such a wide variety of victims that it was never directly associated with sex at all. We knew what it meant, though, in its sexual sense – two blokes doing unspeakable things – and knew that at all costs you did not want to be one. There was nothing and no one to counter that notion, either in my immediate world or in anything I ever saw on television, in a movie, a newspaper, or a book. In the classroom, it simply did not exist. And I didn't care enough to seek anything or anyone out. There was no way in the world I was like that, and as best I could I banished that dream from my mind, and when it happened again, I banished it again, and again. I never told a soul.

I was bewildered rather than tormented, but my confusion didn't dominate my life then, if only because there was not a single other thing about me or my life to suggest I really was *one of those* – whatever *one of those* really was. No one ever used the word *poofter* to describe me. My very nature, or at least the one the rest of the world saw, was my greatest blessing, because poofters surely did not do the things I did – I was physically fearless, strong, rough around the edges, a larrikin, and popular with girls. That marked me not as a poof, but as a player. I looked like one of the most effective seducers at Morisset High, and from the outside it was easy to conclude that I was a precocious 14-year-old pants man.

The truth was, I wasn't doing anything with anyone. I wasn't using girls as a cover, either. At that stage I wasn't even prepared to accept that I *needed* cover. Admitting I needed to hide my true self from the world would have required greater self-awareness and self-acceptance than I'd mustered by then. Deceit would have been a breakthrough of sorts, because it would have meant I had a firm grip on the secret, and that was a long time away. Denial and delusion came first. I tried not to think about that part of me at all – and if I did, I tried to convince myself that whatever dodgy wiring in my brain was making my mind wander down that path, it would fix itself naturally sometime. I thought that perhaps all boys went through this. And perhaps it would change when I actually had sex with a girl – not that I really had much of an idea how to do that, either, and even less physical desire. I was terrified of trying and getting it wrong, a disaster I feared could leave me more messed up than before. I was in no hurry to hasten the experiment.

*

IN THE meantime, the trait of a lifetime was being established as I discovered how easy it was for me to form strong *emotional* bonds with the opposite sex. I found I could talk with girls easily, and them with me. And if I was popular with girls at school, I was completely surrounded by them on weekends at the Cooranbong Pony Club, which became the focus of my life outside school. The apprentice hoodlum who'd ridden the trains in Sydney with a can of spray paint was now a keen member of a statewide organisation whose goal, apart from developing skills in the saddle, was *to promote the highest ideals of sportsmanship, citizenship and loyalty, thereby cultivating strength of character and self-discipline*. I can't pretend I ever thought about it in those terms, or that Pony Club actually instilled all of those things in me, but I loved it. To me Pony Club was about horses and mates, and not just mates – mates who loved horses. *Girls* who loved horses.

I became friends with Melanie Denmark early on. We met at Pony Club, and she invited me for a ride, just the two of us. *Meet me at the top of the hill,* she said, and I did. We rode for hours. I hadn't a clue where we were going, but assumed as the hours went by that she must have been taking me in a circle and that we'd soon loop back to the starting point. She wasn't, and we didn't.

It was getting dark when we finally turned around and I realised we'd been riding more or less in a straight line and had to ride the same distance back to reach home. It would take hours. But as remained true then and later, I figured that if I wasn't worried, no one else needed to be. We were both wearing Drizabones, and decided that if it got too dark to keep going we'd just tie up the horses and sleep out for the night under our coats. We kept riding and eventually made it home that night to find our mums waiting together at Melanie's house, beside themselves with worry. It seemed that, as we were only 14, our mothers didn't share our wisdom and had called the police when we hadn't returned by nightfall. As they'd never met until that night, they at least got a friendship out of it, and so did Melanie and I.

Mel never became my girlfriend – no one did, despite the wealth of opportunity. Eventually I'd fall in love with her, or that's what I thought it was, and when I was 15 I wrote her a letter to tell her so. She was flattered, but nothing came of it – we were *mates*. I think at heart we both knew that then, and still do today. I certainly loved *being* with her, because she loved horses as much as I did and had the same affinity for the outdoors and everything to be found there. She could even catch snakes, and that was enough for me. But relationships like this were as much as I could manage then or for a long time afterwards, and were probably better in their way than anything my male friends were enjoying at the time.

Part of me wanted to be attracted to girls, but part of me was happy that I wasn't. Seeing how other boys at school dealt with girls was enough to put me off. I'd love to have shared their unequivocal sexual attraction, but not one of them was able to develop the friendships that I did. Without knowing it, I was learning that the barriers between men and women are most easily broken down when the possibility of sex is removed from the equation.

Sometime in 1990, our second year in Cooranbong, peer pressure and my general confusion joined forces. At 15, I lost my virginity to an older girl who I barely knew. I felt terrified, but I hoped that it would cure me, and though I managed the act, it was with neither skill nor enjoyment. It felt wrong and, while I was no longer a virgin, it would have been easier to remain one than to live with the guilt, shame and inadequacy I was left to deal with afterwards. I don't know what it meant to her – I was too young, selfish and confused to care.

AT SCHOOL, I was muddling through – neither failing nor excelling, just getting by. Agriculture was the only subject that really grabbed me. I was good at it because I loved it – again, the brain switched on when it saw a reason to. The school had a 10-acre farm where the classroom theory could be put into practice, and we had enough land at home for me to do the same there. I convinced Mum and Dad I needed sheep, goats and chickens to help me do my homework. I did it, too, coming home and setting to work on my own chooks, trying to match the food-to-weight ratios we'd learned. As the end of Year 10 neared, many of my mates were getting ready to leave school to take up a trade. I lost a group of my closest friends to apprenticeships and, given my academic record, I could have joined them. Studying ag was one of the things that kept me going, and it also gave me my proudest moment at Morisset High. People were sometimes shocked and often amused by the amount of mischief I got up to, but they were never more startled than when the school handed out an award for academic excellence and spotted an unfamiliar figure on the stage. It was me, as bewildered as everyone else that I'd finally made it up there.

It was obvious to everyone that animals, especially horses, were my one true passion and one of my teachers suggested I do work experience with Scott Doyle, a vet in a nearby town. Scott and I got along and he asked me to come and work for him on weekends. There was a little money involved, but the largest pay cheque was the experience. I helped Scott with everything from sickly cats to dying horses, sometimes staying over with him and his wife on weekends and going on emergency calls with him in the middle of the night. I had something you can't learn from a book – a natural grasp of the nature of animals, and no fear of them. That was crucial.

Scott was impressed enough to think I had a future in his profession and nudged me in that direction. He wasn't to know just how average my school performance was, and just how comical an idea it was that I could ever put my head down for long enough to get into a veterinary science college, let alone keep it down once I got there. Scott's enthusiasm even survived witnessing the first time I got drunk. I'd invited him and his wife for dinner at home with Mum and Dad. The adults had wine and for the first time I was allowed to join in. I think they believed sensible consumption in polite adult company was better for me than binge sessions on the sly with my mates. *Let him go*, they said. *He'll learn*. Three glasses later, I had. I was thoroughly sick the next morning when I was woken before dawn by a neighbour whose new foal had injured itself crashing into a fence. I called Scott, who came over to find a young horse and a young man who'd both found out there are some things you need to learn the hard way.

I was growing up. At 16, I was already thinking of myself as a third adult in the household. Mum and Dad often had to leave us three kids to our own devices. Dad still had to work in the city, as he would do for years. He was driving trucks and spent Monday to Friday of most weeks staying at Pop's, rather than drive a couple of hours every morning and night. Mum was still hairdressing and the loyal clients she'd built up over years were all in the city, so three days a week she'd make the trip south. She'd normally drive back the same day, but sometimes would stay over with Dad. That meant I was in charge of Sally and Leah, who were 13 and 10.

I've never been sure whether Mum and Dad just didn't understand how irresponsible I could be, or whether they knew, but believed that at heart I had enough sense to stop before the house burned down. Sally and I did let horses into the house more than once – Buddy got through the entrance hall and the kitchen to the hallway – and we had a motorbike indoors, too. A car in the driveway with no adults around was also too much for me to resist. But I stopped short of arson. I was mad more than I was bad, and being mad was a way of keeping being sad at bay. It was my armour.

Life was an adventure then – horseriding, fishing, motorbikes, camping weekends in the mountains with my mates, then back to school where I knew everyone and was involved in everything. If there was mischief, I was a part of it. The outside world saw me as Crazy Adam, and he was someone for me to believe in, too. When I was him, I wasn't that other kid who had strange dreams and wrong thoughts. He also kept me busy, and the busier I was the less time I had to think and dream. Crazy Adam was big and strong enough to swallow the rest of me whole, most of the time. It was a way of staying sane.

But you can only bury yourself so deep. When I was on my own and everything was quiet, even Crazy Adam would have to sit still and give way to the other Adam who was shot through with self-doubt and confusion.

I was lonely, despite having plenty of friends who were boys and plenty of friends who were girls. I had never had a girlfriend, and the idea of having a boyfriend just never occurred to me. Whatever those feelings I was having were, they were only about sex. There was nothing in the world around me to tell me otherwise, to suggest that there could ever be anything more meaningful to it – that two men could fall in love, build a relationship, a life. So even if I was dimly aware that there had to be other people *like that* somewhere, it didn't make me feel any better, because I didn't want to be like *them*. It was ugly and wrong and people hated it, hated them. *I* hated them, whoever they were. The only thing that stopped me completely despising myself was the delusion that there had to be some mistake. Eventually I would come right.

In the meantime I had to live with my secret desires. I couldn't act on them, and even if I'd wanted to, I wouldn't have had a clue where to go or what to do. If it was ever going to happen, if the dreams I'd had were ever going to find expression in real life, it would be by accident. And as much as I wanted it to all go away, part of me wanted that accident to happen. I couldn't talk about my secret. I was convinced no one could ever know, because if they did I would be cut adrift from my entire life. I'd rather have died. But to physically experience it was another thing. The dirty thoughts and dreams disgusted me, but were intensely enjoyable. *What would it really be like?* There was no easy way to find out until, out of nowhere, the accident happened.

We had been swimming, my friend and I, by a creek where no one could see us, and after our swim we started wrestling, play-fighting, flipping each other over and gripping each other's arms and rolling around, and something told me there was more to it than just that. There was for me. Before long I was getting hard, and before long I realised that he was getting hard, too. I could only guess what was going on in his head, but I knew mine was spinning, and that it was wrong but what I wanted.

Nothing happened that day, but it could have and I suspected then that I had a way to find out. So when we were alone together another day, I flicked his ear, hard, and flicked it again, signalling it was time to rumble. We started fighting and the same thing happened again. But this time we didn't just keep wrestling and pretend it wasn't happening. We went from fighting to kissing and then our shirts came off and our pants, and we were naked, and all those disgusting dreams were coming true, except I wasn't disgusted, it *was* what I wanted. We didn't go all the way, but we did enough to give me the answer to the question.

When I got home, I sat down and cried. I hated myself for letting it happen, and thought that if this was really me, how was I ever going to live with myself? I decided it could never be repeated. I already had to live with the terror of people finding out. What if my *parents* found out? I couldn't be certain he would keep our secret. And for a time I felt as if the sin on my face was betraying me anyway – as if people would know just by looking. But in going through that fear and self-hatred I began to develop a skill I would use often from that day on: burying it all so deeply it was hard even for me to reach it. *Get rid of it. Never again.* That was the deal I made with myself. It was not an easy one to reach, because if *that* was off-limits, and if girls were out of bounds, then there was nowhere else for me to go.

When I saw my friend next not a word was said, and never would be. It never happened with him again, or with anyone for a long time.

Chapter 5

I FELT lost. My school days were coming to an end and adulthood loomed, but in so many ways I felt anything but grown up. I was scared and confused, and I wrote it all down, as I often did – a letter to myself, trying to explain me to me, but coming up with nothing. *I am in a type of wonderland at the present time, not knowing what to do, when to do, how to do. I am just not sure what I am actually here for, but I feel soon I will overcome this emptiness.*

I marked the official arrival of adulthood with a party at home – a joint birthday celebration for me, Sally, and two mates. I told Mum there would be 80 people coming, but word spread and 250 turned up and took over the house, drunk and randy. Mum caught one pair rooting in a bedroom, and was so angry at that and the general mayhem that my 18th could easily have become a funeral. But with Mum, the consequences were never as severe as her withering looks and tone suggested. She could put up with a lot, and she did.

But it was time for me to get out of my parents' hair. I had just scraped through my HSC, getting a bare pass that didn't equip me for much. I still had no idea what I was going to do and would probably have wasted a better mark anyway. Early in the new year, I scored a job of sorts with a local window tinter, Bruce. He struck an unusual bargain, employing me in return for providing me with free board and lodging in the home he shared with his girlfriend. Occasionally he would throw me some cash. It wasn't a wage as such, but it was a new life and I jumped at it.

Mum and Dad weren't thrilled, and didn't particularly approve of Bruce, but they must have found some relief in not having to tolerate the stresses I brought to the house. Over the previous two years I'd become harder and harder to live with, taking all my frustrations out at home while staying the life of the party outside it. They were the first to see the angry young man I was becoming. Being surly, cranky and ungrateful didn't set me apart from most other teenagers, but I was worse than most in degree. I had dealt with the pressure to do better at school and the pressure to have a girlfriend by pushing both issues to one side, where I hoped they'd go away. I didn't have to be the smart guy or the guy with a girlfriend if I was something else entirely – Crazy Adam. He was at least an identity, and everyone knew who he was and liked him. Only Mum and

Dad sensed that he might be a walking time bomb with a very short fuse.

Finishing school and moving out of home slightly lengthened the wick. I was independent at last and didn't have to deal with the daily pressures of classroom and family. Even when they weren't asking questions, I was always wondering what my friends and family were thinking about me. Now there were no mates and no Mum to answer to. Not wondering what they were thinking about me meant I could wonder less about myself. After a couple of years of thinking about myself nearly all the time, my brain needed the break.

I learned then how much easier it is for an adult to pretend he's someone else. Independence offers the freedom to fib and hide, and I was mature enough now to do it effectively. As a grown-up I had the right to be mysterious and private, and no one was more grateful for it than me.

The drawback to working was that it meant spending much less time with my horses. I felt too grown up for Pony Club, and my enthusiasm for it had started to fade anyway in the senior years at school. Riding horses while wearing jodhpurs in a club largely made up of horse-loving girls was not what a teenage boy wanted to be seen doing, and this particular teenage boy had even more reason to run a mile from anything that could be called sissy. Over time, what had been my weekend religion became instead just a hobby, and once I was out of home it was a hobby I had less and less time to enjoy.

As the year went on, I worked when Bruce needed me to, fished and rode when I could, and expanded my circle of friends. My pseudo-job came to an end when Bruce's business went under. In an odd twist, however, when life turned sour for Bruce, it looked up for me. He recommended me to a bigger tinting company in Newcastle and, although I had only a few months experience, he must have sold me well because they took me on as their commercial sales manager, gave me a company car and phone and paid me enough that I could rent a flat with some mates and strike out on my own, dependent on no one.

I moved to Bonnells Bay, a five-minute drive from home, renting a flat opposite one shared by a group of friends. I had flatmates of my own who came and went, and was revelling in my freedom. I was still one of the boys, and I was also still surrounded by girls. I never understood that being the bloke who never hit on them or harassed them, the bloke who would always talk to them and listen to their problems, made me more attractive to them, and made them more inclined to apply the one pressure I most wanted to avoid.

In the end I brought it on myself anyway when I went to an office party and ended up in bed that night with a woman. It wasn't especially memorable, but in doing it I gave myself an unexpected whack across the head: in this, my first sexual encounter as an adult, I had managed to perform. How well I performed I'll never know, because I had nothing much to compare it to then or later, but everything at least worked as it was supposed to and I didn't need to ask for a map and a torch to find my way. That was enough to make me wonder if I couldn't make a serious go of being *normal*, though I knew that the other thing had not faded away.

So, from that one encounter, I took a little relief, some more confusion and a temporary suit of armour against whispers and doubts. People knew what I'd done. Worried as always about what others might be thinking of me, at least now I'd given them something concrete to think about. The pressure eased. For the first time in ages, I felt I was not going to detonate any time soon. I couldn't have been more wrong.

AS THEY always had been, weekends were for the outdoors, doing something physical – fishing, riding bikes or horses, taking a boat out on Lake Macquarie. One day in late December, some mates and I spent the afternoon waterskiing, as we often did. Adam Gosden, a local, was out and about that day, too, driving with his younger sister, Arlea. He lived near me and had attended the same high school, though he left before I started. He was six years my senior. We might have passed each other on the street once, or driven down the same road. But we'd never met, and I knew nothing of him then. It was many years before I would hear the story that turned him into something more than a ghost.

Adam's father, Ron, was a coalminer who'd suffered from heart disease since he was forty. Adam was the oldest of five children, and was told by his father, *Look after your mother and your brothers and sisters when I'm gone*. Ron died at 56, when Adam was only in his early twenties, and Adam accepted the responsibility his father had given him, though his mother feared he was too young. He embraced his new role and shared his mother's load, becoming best friend and mentor to his siblings. He was a boilermaker by trade, then became a fireman.

Like me, he loved the outdoors – camping, cycling and trips away. But he had been forced to confront responsibility in a way that I never had. That afternoon he was doing something his father might have done: running an errand with his little sister. He turned a corner, and there I was, coming the other way.

Everything changed forever then. It was a Sunday, a sunny afternoon that had not been notable for anything. I'd had a hundred Sundays like it, save for the mistake I made at the end. I don't remember seeing him at all. It was a corner I turned every day on my way to work, with a Give Way sign and not enough traffic to ever make you wary. A stop sign might have saved him. There is one there now, but that doesn't make me feel any better. I was an accident waiting to happen.

Those days water-skiing on the lake were always accompanied by beer drinking – slow and drawn out and more to quench the thirst than to get drunk, because we were there to ski and ski well. When that was over, we'd take the boat home and wind down in the late afternoon, with drinks and an early meal. That afternoon we decided to get pizza. My flatmate Troy and I went to pick it up. I drove. We were talking about the day we'd just had, recalling mishaps on the water as one skier or another took a tumble. I wasn't speeding. I didn't think I was drunk. We hadn't gone a kilometre when we got to the corner, and I don't remember seeing him at all. It's a blur now, just as it was then.

I remember the impact. He was turning right into the street I was leaving, turning left but turning too wide. My car came to a stop on the other side of the street and I remember getting out of the car in a daze from the force of the crash. There was hardly a scratch on me. I remember people coming out of their houses and by the time I was making my way back across the road towards him there were people around his car, in his car. I remember thinking I would go over to help him, because he wasn't out of his car yet and I knew first aid so I thought that if he was hurt I could help. And that was the moment when it happened, when everything changed. The man held me back in the middle of the road, and made me stop.

I remember he said: *Just go away, mate. This guy's gone. He's gone.*

*

NOTHING HAS ever seemed so unreal. The world turned white, like it was raining ash. I couldn't see and I couldn't speak and I remember sitting on the side of the road, crouching on the spare tyre that had been thrown loose from the back of my van, and as I sat there I picked up dirt in my hand and started eating it. I can't remember speaking to anyone else, or seeing anything else, just my vision being consumed by a storm of white and eating dirt and hearing the crash, over and over, and the man saying, over and over, *Just go away, mate*. Bang. *He's gone*. Bang. *He's gone*. Bang. *He's gone*.

At moments the noises and voices stopped, along with everything else, and time was frozen white. An ambulance took me to the hospital, where I was diagnosed with shock, not a broken bone to be found. There would be no lasting damage at all. But I'd never felt more like dying.

At the hospital a nurse told my parents I was refusing to see anyone, that I was suicidal. When I finally agreed to see them, Mum, at a loss for what to say, offered prayer. Dad, who had never spoken to me about Vietnam, did so then. He told me he knew how it felt to have death on your conscience. *But you didn't go out today intending to kill someone.*

I couldn't take anything in. There was no room in my head for anything other than the bang and the words. I'd killed a man. *Just go away, mate. He's gone.*

They took blood for testing, but let me go home that night, even let me keep my licence. He was dead, while I was home in my bed, dead inside. I couldn't feel yet what I'd done because I couldn't believe it had happened and I couldn't remember it, and the bang and the words were like a dream that kept bouncing around and around in my head, telling me what I'd done but too insane to be real. Bang. *He's gone.*

The next morning I went to work, still in a daze, and the radio was on and I heard the news. The news was about me, and him, the two Adams. *A man was killed yesterday,* the radio said, and I remember they got it wrong. They said it happened at traffic lights, but suddenly it was real anyway and it didn't matter *how* it had happened. It was true. I walked outside and sat down and cried so hard I could hardly stand up again. My legs were giving way, and I said to my workmate Andrew, through the tears, *I can't finish this job,* and he drove me home and there wasn't a moment for a long time to come that the thought didn't wander freely through my mind.

Just go away, mate. He's gone.

It was four days before Christmas.

Chapter 6

THE LOST year began then. The phone rang after Christmas and it was Senior Constable Graham Beames from the Newcastle Accident Investigation Squad. I had to go to Morisset police station to make a statement, he said. He was a cog in the machine that would now take over my life.

In those early days, I had good grounds to fear the worst. I believed that I deserved the worst, but it didn't make it any easier to contemplate. There seemed a real chance I would be charged with manslaughter, a charge that could have put me away for 14 years.

I went to the station to make my statement and Constable Beames took down my words. He was kind, as the police I dealt with always were. The charge would be serious, but not as awful as I'd feared: culpable driving under the influence, causing death, which carried a maximum sentence of seven years. I learned just how intoxicated I'd been that day. My blood alcohol reading was 0.160, more than three times the legal limit. A court date was set and I was told I was free to go, but all I wanted to do was lock myself away.

The cloud over my head settled like a heavy blanket, smothering everything inside me and not letting anything in or out. I was already good at hating myself and at trying to hide it, and Adam's death only gave me more reasons to pile fresh hatred upon the loathing. Nobody knew what to say to me, and I was in no mind to hear even the wisest of words.

I hated myself to the core and shut everyone out, including my family. In response, they tried to put me in a box and wrap me in tissue, flooding me with understanding and kindness and tolerance and love, perhaps thinking I'd be safer thrashing around with all that human warmth to protect me. I would just bounce against it, taking it all without gratitude, becoming more withdrawn and more angry. All they did then was give me more.

The more my family gave, the more I rejected them. That was how the next nine months passed, in a permanent, angry daze. I'd gone from not knowing what to do with my life to not knowing if I could keep on living it. I was disintegrating inside, and my family bore the brunt. I moved home soon after the accident, and it was as if I'd said to them, *You think I was difficult before? Watch me now.* I snarled and rebelled and pushed them away and told them to leave me alone. I didn't want to be coddled, because I didn't deserve it and I didn't want to hear that everything would be okay because I knew it wouldn't. They let me go, appeased me, never tried to pull me into line or told me to calm down or show some respect. Mum and Dad told my sisters, *Tread carefully around Adam, he's going through a lot.*

I didn't tell them, or anyone, that I was spending hours mulling over different ways to commit suicide, but Mum and Dad knew well enough how fragile I was. I'd been seeing a counsellor from the time of the accident, and while it helped to talk to someone, it never really seemed to make me feel any better. My parents and sisters were seeing another counsellor – the accident had shattered us all – and Mum and Dad took expert advice that we should all seek professional guidance.

For Dad, it was the start of a remarkable journey of his own, because it marked the first time he'd really talked openly to anyone about his experiences in Vietnam. His son's tragedy forced him to confront his own. He was stronger for it, and both he and Mum needed to be that year. They had me on a permanent suicide watch, eyeing every move and mood. Mum would come into my bedroom at night to check I was still there and still breathing. It was the cruellest of punishments for a mother already confronting the awfulness of what her son had done, and the punishment that might await him. I didn't – couldn't – think of her and Dad, and what it might be doing to them. I rejected them every day. *I don't want your love.* I believed they would all be better off without me.

I banished friends. I thought about death. I feared prison. I wrestled with the guilt, and the guilt always won. At night sometimes, I'd cry myself to sleep thinking about Adam, even talking to him, and telling him I wished it was me who'd died and not him, that I wished I could take it back, swap places, bring him home to his family and take me from mine instead.

I tried nearly always to be alone, and that took me back to my horses, and not for the first or last time they were the ones I could talk to. I'd take long rides on my own and tell them what had happened and how I felt and what I was thinking of doing. They were who I talked to then, my horses and the man I had killed, and for a long time it was only with them that I was brave enough to cry.

During the days, I kept working. It seemed futile, given that whatever way I looked at it I had no future, but it was a routine and it meant I could get out of the house and turn my brain off. Otherwise, there was just the waiting, for me or the legal system to do its worst. Three times I went to Wallsend Local Court, and three times it was deferred, so we'd go home where I could continue to think of ways to die and keep punishing my parents. It had already been decided I would acknowledge my responsibility – how could I do anything else? – and on the fourth appearance, when they finally read out the charge and asked for my plea, I told them, and it was written down, at last official. *Guilty*.

After that it was a matter of waiting again for the

sentencing hearing, where a judge would weigh my case before deciding what would become of me. The date was set for 29 September, nine months after the accident. *You'll get community service,* people told me. *You're young. No prior convictions.* I still don't know whether they believed it, or were just trying to make me feel better, but I knew it was rubbish. I knew I would go to prison. Given what I'd done, it was only a question of how long I'd be gone.

THE DECISION I made to kill myself was gradual. I'd despised the secret part of myself for long enough, though in those months since the accident I hadn't thought about my other ugly truth much at all. It had not gone away. It was just overwhelmed by everything else; it had joined with my guilt over Adam's death to form a mass of loathing and shame. This was beyond the reach of denial or delusion or deceit. I couldn't pretend it wasn't happening now, that it might go away, that it was all a mistake that would right itself. I had only one card left.

Am I here? Or am I not here?

It was the only decision I could still control; the power over my own life or death, the only power no one could take away from me. I'd spent a long time thinking about how I might do it, the ways that would hurt the most and the ways I might fail. I was more terrified of failing than succeeding. But I came home one day, in the week before I was to be sentenced, and knew this was the day I would do it. I was running out of time and if I was going to play my card it had to be now. I wrote a note, saying why and saying sorry and saying goodbye. Then I said to my sister, *I'm going for a walk*.

I left home and walked to the mountains, to a place I'd been to so many times before with my horses and my mates. It was a place I thought of as mine. There was a ledge there on the edge of a gorge where I'd sat so many times, where you could be alone and think about anything.

I cried as I walked up there, hurrying because I wanted it to be done and over. I sat on the ledge and the tears were a flood by then as I talked to myself through the torrent, screaming out sometimes, then going quiet and saying goodbye to everyone in my head one last time because I knew this was it and I had to make what peace I could before I went over.

A sound cut through the noise of my screams. A bird singing. Its song caught me, and I looked up to see it was small and sitting on the branch of a nearby tree. The bird looked back and kept singing, and my tears kept running down. I was looking at it and smiling at a passing moment of life and beauty and joy. I laughed and cried so hard that it blinded me, and when I could see again I looked up and the bird was gone. I couldn't explain it then. I can't explain it now. But that moment saved me. I couldn't do it any more. I stood up and ran home, to burn the note I'd written earlier.

There was no need to say goodbye now. In that moment, peering through tears at a bird singing on a mountain, I'd decided to stay, and I knew I would get through whatever came next.

DAD TOOK the stand and spoke to the judge, telling him about Vietnam and how death can haunt you for life.

He will live with what he's done for the rest of his days.

He hoped the judge would agree that that was punishment enough. But I knew I would not be coming home again. Some mates had come up, believing they would be there to walk me outside when it was all over. Even my lawyer had told us that I would get community service, but I didn't believe him, and I didn't want it to be true. No one knew more than I just how guilty I was: the guilt that had consumed me for nine months went way beyond any legal definition of the word. I didn't need the court to add to it with a slap on the wrist. As I stood there that day waiting to be sentenced, I wanted to lose my freedom, if only to find a way that I could live with it again.

They handcuff you when it's all over, and lead you back through the court and down the stairs to the cells and it starts right there. You're a prisoner from the second the words hit the courtroom floor. Eighteen months, the judge said, with a minimum of six. *The earliest day on which the offender may be eligible to be released on parole is 29 March 1995.*

Sally screamed and cried when she heard it. *No, no, no.* Mum and Dad wept and, as they led me away, their son now a prisoner in a suit and tie and handcuffs, they tried to reach out and hug me, but I just wanted to go. There was relief, and if there was also fear I wasn't about to show it then. I'd received what I deserved.

They took me down to the police cells and put me in a pen on my own. A policeman came in, carrying my case file, and I could see the words: *Adam Sutton. Suicidal.* He took away my tie, belt and shoelaces and left me alone again until Dad came down. Dad tried to be as strong as he could, but he still couldn't hold back the tears. I told him I was okay, that I would be okay and not to worry. I refused to let my own tears flow. I'd been cutting myself adrift from them for months, and now it felt complete – for the first time, my parents were utterly helpless to do anything for me, and I knew it. We spent 10 minutes together before they made Dad leave. Then I was alone again, but I'd felt alone even when he was with me.

They left me there in the cell for two hours, then came and took me outside to the prison van. I was on my way to jail. In three weeks I'd be turning 20.

Chapter 7

THEY DIDN'T tell me where I was going. I was caged on my own on one side of the van, separated from the older, more serious criminals, but they could see me through the wire and they banged and yelled at me as we drove from the courthouse to wherever I was headed for my first night. I said nothing back, not flinching or crying even when they told me what terrible things might await someone young, blond and innocent like me. The drive seemed to last an age. But I had to keep fear at bay.

Finally we arrived: Maitland maximum security prison. What was I doing here? Maitland was home to the worst of the worst. It was a sandstone relic of another age, built in the mid-1800s. Sixteen men had been hanged there; when I arrived, prisoners who might once have faced the noose lived out their lives there instead.

The other prisoners were taken out first, leaving me

cuffed in the cage for 20 minutes, then two officers came and escorted me in. It was well dark by then. They handed my paperwork to an officer inside, who read it, then looked at them and started talking about me as if I wasn't there.

We've got nowhere to put him!

Put him in there.

No, we can't put him in there.

They didn't know what I was doing there either, and were looking for somewhere I'd be safe. They settled on a cell and gave me my first order: *Strip.* I stripped to my underpants. *Get them off too.* I was naked.

An officer pointed to a box in the corner full of green uniforms. *Find one that fits you and take a spare.*

I dressed and was given a red plastic plate covered in foil and ordered to follow the officer to the cells, which were all locked for the night by then. He opened one, pushed the steel door ajar, and without a word pushed me in and locked the door behind me.

I stood there in total darkness. I couldn't see the door or a wall or another person, and froze until a voice said, *If you put your hand down to the left, you'll feel a bunk. That's your bed.*

I did what he said and felt the mattress. I sat down and pushed my red plate with uneaten food under the bunk. There was not another word spoken. I lay there, frozen again, eyes open, silent, terrified in the blackness that felt like it would never end.

Hours passed and as the sun rose a streak of light squinted through the tiny window and I could start to make out my surroundings – a small cell, four metres by six, with three bunks stacked on each side, a man in each one. There was one sink and one toilet.

Finally a voice. *So, you're the new kid?*

Yes.

A man got down from a bunk above me and moved to the toilet, pulled down his pants and took a shit, there in the open because that was what you had to do. The toilet was squashed in a corner against the end of the lower bunk opposite mine. Someone roused at him for getting up too early. The man on the toilet ignored them, and looked at me.

What are you in for?

I got into trouble.

We're all in trouble in here, mate.

THEY FOUND me a bed in the young offenders wing, where the prisoners were all under 24 and segregated from the other inmates. For most of us, Maitland was a stop-off point on the way to somewhere else, a place where we could be assessed and then dispatched to another jail. That morning, I didn't care which jail I went to, I just wanted to know what I was supposed to do in this one. I knew nothing, and was too scared to ask anything, so I waited and watched and hoped I'd learn fast.

A trolley came past the cell door and we were let out to retrieve a bowl of porridge or milk and a small box of cereal. Then we were let out into the yards. The main offenders were kept in their yard, the young offenders in ours, but the two yards were divided only by wire, and you could watch them and they could watch you and talk to you if they wanted to.

Everyone looked as if they knew what they were doing. Some were talking. Some were walking, doing laps around the yard. I sat down on a bench on my own and tried to look as if I knew how to do that until someone spoke to me briefly, the happiest moment of that first morning. Then another man spoke to me, and said, *You shouldn't be talking to him*. He took me for a walk and explained there was a reason the other prisoner was the first to talk to me; it was because no one else would talk to him. I can't remember why he was off-limits, but it was my first lesson. *Be careful who you talk to. Don't talk to people with enemies.*

That afternoon I had a shower, my first since leaving home to go to court the morning before. They took all six of us from the cell and locked us in the shower block with two shower heads between us. I learned I would never do anything in private, not even take a shit. I'd never crapped in public before. Here there would be five other men lying or sitting nearby watching and listening. It was two days before I was brave enough to do it.

It was a weekend, and Sunday was visitors' day. The last time Mum and Dad had seen me I was handcuffed in a suit. This time I was effectively in a straitjacket – a pair of overalls with no sleeves, my arms confined so I couldn't use my hands. Before each visit you had to remove your normal uniform for a strip search – lift your balls, bend over – then they'd put you in the overalls before you could see your visitors. I went out to them, to a room full of small plastic tables and chairs, still determined to keep my guard up. I couldn't have begun to explain any of it to them anyway, and if I'd tried it would only have worried them more, so I told them again that I was okay. *Don't worry about me.*

I could see in their eyes that they didn't believe me. None of us knew what to say. There was a part of me that didn't want to see them at all and part of me that didn't want them to leave when it was over. A guard told us our time was up. I wasn't theirs any more, and all I could offer them were the same useless few words. *Don't worry about me. I'm okay.*

Strangely enough I was okay, or as okay as I could expect given where I was. I thought that once I got on top of the rules and routines – the official ones set by the guards and the unofficial ones set by the prisoners – I would adapt and survive. By now I was a master at pretending to be someone I wasn't, and at pretending to be happy when I was anything but. I thought those qualities would stand me in good stead in a place where front was everything. I had quickly learned it was not a question of not being scared – fear went with the territory – the key was never to let anyone *see* you were scared, because this was a pack that thrived on exploiting weakness wherever they could find it.

As the days went by, I found the official rules were set in stone and easy to follow. There were no tricks, just times and places and things you had to do. Prison excuses you from ever having to make a decision. You wake, sleep, eat, shower, exercise and work at the same time every day and there are guards and steel doors and gates and fences to make sure you do what you're supposed to do, when you're supposed to do it. You're a rat in a wheel. The unofficial rules you pick up as you go. If you've seen a prison movie, it wouldn't take you long to work them out. There are drugs and sex and violence in jail, weak men and strong ones, good screws and bad. A lot of it *is* just like a movie. It makes everything weirdly familiar.

After my first week I was given a job as a cleaner in the prison hospital, a position prized because it offered access to the drug cabinet. The drugs were locked away, but as soon as word spread that I was working there the pressure was on me to score. I resisted it, but knew that couldn't last. I would be damned if I did and damned if I didn't, and I couldn't be sure which fate would be worse.

Next I was propositioned for sex, not aggressively but enough to make me think that the threats and warnings I'd heard in the back of the prison van could easily come true.

Like everything else in prison, rape does not just happen in the movies. And the violence can be brutal. One morning I saw a prisoner beat another's face to a pulp with a dumbbell, not stopping till his victim didn't have a nose left.

It really wasn't a prison for a young first offender jailed over a car accident. To understand that, you only had to know who was in the dog yard, as we called the exercise area for the worst prisoners, who were kept even more segregated for their own protection. Ivan Milat, the notorious backpacker serial killer, was in there, as was John Glover, Sydney's granny killer. I'd hear the names and recognise them from the news and wonder how I'd ended up under the same roof as men like those. But I didn't tell the officers that when they called me in after two weeks and said I would have to leave the jail. *You don't belong here,* I was told. *You should be in minimum security.*

I resisted. I felt I knew this place and understood it. I had some mates. I believed it was cruel to make me face another jail, other rules, other prisoners. It had been hard enough coming to this one, but I'd done it and thought I could make it work. *Don't make me do it all over again.*

But they did. I was removed from my cell, put in a bus, handcuffed to the seat in front of me and driven from Maitland jail. They closed the place four years later – it was too old and rundown, unfit even for the worst of the worst. It had been open for 145 years, home to infamous prisoners, notorious escapees, convicts shipped from England and young men like me. I was there for less than three weeks. I'd turn 20 somewhere else.

THE PRISON system makes some allowance for circumstance, youth and hope. I was sent to St Helier's Correctional Centre, a minimum security prison farm in Muswellbrook that housed offenders like me. Some inmates had been in maximum security but were nearing the end of their sentences and needed to be slowly re-introduced to the daily grind of 'normal' life. It was hardly what you'd call summer camp, unless your summer camp involves strip searches and drug raids and lockdowns at night. But as much as I'd been reluctant to move, I was relieved once I got there. There were about 200 prisoners kept in different wings, which were essentially two-storey houses with 10 rooms in each. There were two beds in each room, a common kitchen for each wing, and communal showers and toilet blocks. It was relief enough that here I'd be able to wash and crap in private. Having survived the weeks in Maitland, being here seemed a doddle.

I was checked in, taken to my wing and shown to my room. It was time to start learning again. It didn't take me long, mainly because I found good teachers. On my third day, I met Sam Dixon, who was 10 years older and 100 years wiser, with a string of convictions to his name for things like break-and-enter and drug possession but a kind heart and a watchful eye. We met because once again I was talking to someone who was better left alone. Sam rescued me and told me to come with him. He was good-looking, muscular and knew everything there was to know about this prison and several others. Depending on your point of view, he was either the best or worst teacher I could have had.

To my mind, Sam was the one who helped me survive it all. He gave me the confidence to know what was right and what was wrong. The rights and wrongs were different from any I'd known before, but I needed to understand them to get through my time at St Helier's. In prison you're forced to obey two sets of rules, the prison's and the prisoners'. The art is to navigate those waters and avoid the rocks on either side. Sam captained my ship.

We became mates fast and under his guidance I threw myself into an exercise program, jogging and lifting weights, and quickly becoming as fit as I'd ever been. The prison was also a working farm, and as soon as I was allowed to work I took a job outdoors, reconnecting with the land for the first time in many months. I was only working in the chaff mill but it was good enough, and not to be taken for granted – work was a privilege, and I earned $11.80 a week sewing and stuffing bags of chaff that were sent out of the prison for sale. My nickname was Farm Boy. I even took up handicrafts, becoming an expert at making wooden cigarette lighter holders, which became gifts for people on the outside. It sounds like I was being healthy, sensible and responsible and most of the time I was, but I knew that for my time in prison to be bearable I could never forget the other set of rules I had to live by. It made life much simpler to be one of the boys, and that entailed being involved in a certain amount of mischief. I'd never needed much encouragement, and in prison it was all but compulsory.

Sam was in a different wing and before long I'd asked to transfer there so we could share a room. He introduced me to Jim, who was a decade older again and even more of a prison regular than Sam. He told me once that he was institutionalised, meaning he'd been in and out of jail so long he could hardly remember anything else, and it was the one place he functioned effectively. One thing he and Sam both understood was that the jail walls could only restrict your imagination, not kill it entirely.

There were ways and means of doing many banned things in prison, including brewing illicit alcohol, and I was a keen student. We'd drain the sugary syrup from tins of fruit, put the syrup in a bottle, add spoons of Vegemite for its yeast content and sugar, then leave it to ferment. Because I worked on the farm, my main task was to smuggle the concoction from the wing to a hiding place outdoors where the smell wouldn't be noticed, then smuggle it back in when it was ready to drink. Strictly speaking, it never was. Before we could guzzle it, the brew was strained through a sock, and by the time it reached your lips it was so pungent you couldn't drink it without holding your nose. It would make us sick or drunk, or both, and was generally so awful I think the greatest buzz came simply from getting away with it.

In any case, home brew was the mildest of the substances being abused. Prisons are awash with drugs, finding their way in hidden in everything from a visitor's underpants, to tennis balls or dead birds tossed over the fence. Dope was the most popular, and on weekends after visiting hours the entire prison would be abuzz with deals being struck as the smuggled supply worked its way through the dorms. Harder drugs were less common, but there if you wanted them. The kindest thing Sam and Jim ever did for me was protect me from my own stupidity when I saw several other prisoners using heroin. I was young, stupid, naïve, and could take the desire to be one of the crowd a step too far. My two protectors wouldn't let me near it, and if that was the only thing they'd ever done for me, it still would have made them two of the best friends I ever had.

I CAME to think of Sam as a brother. We did everything together, and he became that figure you cannot survive prison without: the man you can trust with your life. We'd talk for hours, and he'd tell me where he'd been and how he'd got trapped in the system and how he was going to take a new path when he got out next time. It would be different, he said. He was going to leave it all behind and make a new start. We even made plans for the things we'd do together when we were both free. We'd go places, start a business. From what I knew of his history, I didn't know whether to believe him, but I hoped it was true, for my sake as much as his.

I grew attached to Sam so quickly I believed I was going to need him outside as much as I did inside. And for all he did for me, I sensed he needed to *belong* to something, or someone. He'd been in jail for such a long time that he rarely received visitors or letters, and because I was getting a constant stream of both I shared my bounty with him. I arranged for Sally to write to him from outside, and he'd join me on weekends when my family and friends came for visits in the garden.

Compared to Maitland, visits were relaxed and easier on both prisoner and visitor. You were still strip-searched, but there was no straitjacket. Visits could last for up to five hours and there was a barbecue in the garden; visitors would come laden with food for a prison picnic. There wasn't a weekend that someone did not come to see me, and usually I'd have people arrive on both Saturday and Sunday. It sounds like a blessing, but it could be a curse. I was envied by the prisoners who had no one, and I knew it. Wanting to be one of the boys, it was not part of my survival plan to be the boy who stood out, and there were times I wished that people outside cared less.

As time went on, visits could sometimes be strained – I often didn't want to be there, and usually had nothing much to say. When every day is almost exactly like the one before it, your conversation runs thin, and the most interesting things about prison life were not things I could share. With Mum and Dad, I was calmer than before and not as inclined to rebuff them at every turn, but there were times I ended visits early in boredom or frustration. I could still be that cruel to them, even telling Mum once, *I don't want you coming here every weekend*. But they were experts by then in dealing with the rocks I hurled their way, and the visits never stopped.

That Christmas, Mum and Dad arrived with Sally, Leah and Nan – Nan, who'd growled at me since I was a brat of a kid but who now wrote to me constantly and prayed that God would take care of me. Mum brought a Christmas spread in a hamper, and we sat in the visitors' area and tried to make it as much like Christmas as we could. Sam didn't have anyone visiting him even on this of all days, so he came to lunch with me. Mum and Dad never judged him, just accepted him as my friend. I'm not sure whether they would have liked him more or less if they also understood that in a way he'd come to replace them. Through no fault of their own, they were powerless to do anything for me. Sam was my protector, supporter, adviser and guide. He'd quickly become family.

There was never anything more to it than that. I was in no doubt that Sam cared for me, and I loved him back. But he was straight, and in any case it remained a bridge I couldn't cross. I hadn't touched another man since that single episode during high school, and though my mind wandered to it in prison, I never came close to acting on those desires. The irony was rich. I was now permanently in the company of young men, which left me in no doubt as to which direction my physical attractions led. Even more conveniently, I was in a place where men had sex with each other because it was the only outlet they had. It had no other meaning, and it didn't suggest you were gay. I could have done it and been confident no one would have thought less of me. But I couldn't, perhaps because to me it *did* have meaning and I still couldn't face what it might be. Paradoxically, I was busy forming my first real relationships with other men. Sam and I were living together and, short of sleeping together, we were as close as two men could be. Without realising it, I was learning how deep the emotional bonds could run and that two men really could love each other. It would take me many years to understand how to apply that wisdom.

It couldn't last, though. Nothing in prison ever does. Early in the new year, Sam was up for parole. He didn't get it, but he was transferred to another jail. In prison, you're supposed to learn not to care, but for all Sam had taught me, I was too young and vulnerable to follow that rule when he left. I'd lost my best mate, and it hurt. Laura Ciszek, a friend from school, was visiting me the day he left the prison. She wrote to me later: *I watched you, Adam, that day we were there and your mate yelled out 'Sam's gone!' You should have seen the look on your face, it was like a part of you had just been taken away*. It had and I couldn't hide it.

Leigh Maule, a girl I'd met in my last year at school, had also become a good friend before jail and a closer one while I was inside. She visited and wrote regularly, and knew how much Sam meant to me. *Things may hurt at times,* she wrote after he'd left, *but always think no matter what it is, that things are always meant for a reason.* There were times, though, when I struggled to see what the reason could be for many of the things I was having to face.

IT WAS the height of summer, and Muswellbrook baked. I was lean, fit, tanned and felt perhaps too much at home. I was managing to juggle the rules of the prisoners and the prison well enough to avoid serious trouble with either, until I answered back to a screw who was trying to break up a fight. He told me to hold my tongue and I gave him a shove. I was cuffed, taken to the senior guard and lost all privileges for 21 days. That meant denial of all pleasurable activities, down to and including the playing of musical instruments. Since I didn't play a musical instrument, I was unfazed by that, but it also included a ban on all visits for three weeks. I didn't much care about that either, but it was my mother's lowest ebb.

Sally wrote to berate me:

What the hell is going on? What have you done? Mum is absolutely devastated, she is so sad. It's like you went back to jail all over again. I know we don't know what it's like in there. It's probably not a very nice place at all. But for Mum's and Dad's sake please try and stay out of shit. They are so worried about you. Mum came into my room on Friday night at about 3 am bawling her eyes out. She is so distressed, she won't work or anything, so please think of how they feel. We do everything we possibly can for you. We all care about you so much, Adam, some people are thinking, well, he mustn't like his visits very much if he is doing stuff to have them taken off him. Heaps of people were looking forward to seeing you. I'm not having a go at you, I just care about you and I want you home on the 29th of March and no later.

MUM COULD only wonder most of the time what I was up to inside, and some of it would have sent her to an early grave. It still might when she reads this book. But I generally took the attitude that telling her even the most basic details of prison life was only going to hurt her more. More pain seemed pointless, especially when she was powerless to change a single thing. My reckless nature was far beyond repair, and one afternoon that summer I came close to dying behind bars.

It was a stinker and we'd cleaned out a wheelie bin and

filled it with water, turning it into a swimming pool that could hold exactly one grown man at a time. I charged at the bin at a run, leaping into the water head first. When my head reached the narrower bottom of the bin, however, it got stuck. My neck was jammed. My arms were jammed. My feet were flailing out the top. The bin was full of water, too heavy to knock over. Unable to move or breathe, for several seconds I was convinced I'd die. Then another prisoner, Dave, a gentle giant of a man, grabbed me by the ankles, hauled me out with one swift tug, threw me to the ground, and told me I was a fucking idiot.

Mum once wrote to me:

> *I'll try not to worry, but that's the way mothers are and you will always be my little Adam no matter how old or big or tough you are. I do realise life is different for you and that you are restricted and denied in a way that makes one angry and only you can deal with that to your best ability. But!! I do have to let you know I always feel safe in the thought that you know what you're doing and think carefully about your actions. Adam, I have great faith in you so please remember, 'that's a mother for you'. Honestly, would you expect me any different?*

For his part, Dad struggled to find ways to get through to me, knowing there were things I wasn't telling them and fearing what those things might be. After one visit, he wrote:

Last week when we saw you on Saturday you didn't look too happy and I asked you a couple of times if anything was wrong and obviously you were not going to say anything but if you feel you have something to say and don't want Mum to hear, write to me and talk about it or maybe just tell me to shut up. You looked as though you were worried about something or someone looking at everything that was going on. I'm here as a friend first and a father second.

Dad knew what it was to wait for the day they let you go home. *When we see you next,* he wrote towards the end of the letter, *it will only be two weeks to go. I used to count down the weeks to go getting out of Vietnam. Somebody didn't tell me about the days.*

And then there was Nan, who would write to tell me she was thinking of me every waking minute of the days:

I know you don't want us to get soppy, so I'll just say that my thoughts and prayers are with you, all the time, whatever I am doing. Keep your chin up, darling, and even though you will come back to us wiser and maybe tougher, don't change, Adam, or try not to – stick to your own principles and morals, which I know have always been good.

Nan would end each letter: *God bless you, and keep you safe for us all.*

Letters came by the dozen, scrawled, awkward notes from male friends alongside long, descriptive letters from girls who signed off with smiley faces or love hearts and drew pictures of flowers on every page. As with the visits, often people did not know what to say, and so they'd just describe their ordinary days outside, going to work or to the pub or to a party. Relationships ended and new ones began, people hated their jobs and fought with their parents, ran into so-and-so at the supermarket or won a netball game on Saturday. I read them all, and was never sure how they were supposed to make me feel. Was this the life I was supposed to go back to? I'd never felt more remote from the world they were describing. But I was at least in no doubt that when freedom came, I'd be walking out to family and friends who loved me and wanted me home.

Then came the letter that defeated me, because I had no words then to match its generosity of spirit. Adam Gosden's sister, who had been in the car with him when he died, was only 14 when she wrote to me.

Adam,
Well, it's about time I wrote this to sort things out. Look, I am sorry that you had to go to jail for six months and live with it for the rest of your life. Anyway, I am Arlea, the girl who was in the car when you hit it. So I know what it's like to have to live with it, I seen what happened to my brother and a normal girl would hate you for it. But

I don't cause I've now realised that it was the alcohol which killed my brother, not you. As long as you don't drink any more I hope we can call it troops, OK! You can either write back or just forget about this letter. It's up to you.
Hopefully friends,
Arlea

Arlea was at high school with my sister Leah at the time she wrote the letter, but I'd never met her or any of Adam Gosden's family. I didn't expect them to forgive me, least of all the young girl who had seen her brother die and who might have died herself that day. A braver man, a man who'd made peace with himself, would have taken the hand being offered to him. But I was too scared, guilty and ashamed. It was a step that would have to wait for another day.

MY SENTENCE was only six months, and while it seemed to last much longer, the end came in a rush. I survived my run-in with the screw without any effect on my sentence, so 29 March 1995 was the day they would have to let me go. As it drew closer, I still had no idea what I was going to do when I got out and knew only that I couldn't pick up life where I'd left it. I was determined to leave Cooranbong. Being reunited with Sam Dixon was what I really wanted most, but I had to wonder if it would happen. He'd been moved to Maitland prison, the jail I'd spent my first weeks in, and was hoping his parole would be granted later that year.

By this stage I was physically and emotionally bruised. The jail had been shaken by a prison-wide raid by officers in search of drugs and other contraband, and I'd been hurt in a minor brawl on another occasion. I was tiring from the strain, scared of what lay ahead, and my head was filled with Sam. I talked about him so often in letters and during visits that I didn't even have to use his name. Everyone else knew who *he* was. Two school friends, Charlie McAskill and her boyfriend Ken Rockley, had moved to Cairns, and I planned to join them there when I got out. I wrote to them two weeks before my release.

> *My writing is up the shit at the moment cause I've fractured two of my fingers and broken my big toe. It's a long story to put on paper, it was to do with me and a few mates who had a problem with some other fellas. Bit worse for wear but you get that. Can't wait to get out of this hole of a place, it's been running fairly hectic lately, everyone went around pulling out and ripping up the gardens today cause they didn't get what they wanted, just trivial shit. But there's been some crazy stuff going on. Thank god I've only got under two weeks. I am going to come up to be with you guys as soon as I can if that's cool. Still don't really know what I want, it's such a mystery to me at the moment. I know I want to be back this way in August*

cause that's when he gets out and me and him have made a few plans that I would like to see come together, it's up to him if he wants to make a go of it or not. He's finishing off four years and has no one to walk out to. I told him I would be there for him.

I'd made that promise before Sam was transferred to Maitland, and repeated it in a long letter I wrote to him in early March. With barely a week to go to my release, he wrote back, leaving me in no doubt about how much he cared but giving me permission to leave and make a go of my own life.

Adam, I have to tell you not to worry about waiting around for me. But if you're around by all means I'll come and stay a while with ya. Plant a few seeds, try our luck hey! Looking forward to it. It's getting to be a worry to see if I can really live a normal life out there. Believe me I'll give it one hell of a shot. Don't be drinking and driving out there either, don't want to see ya back here before I get out.

Would I ever be back inside? The only sure thing prison equips you for is a life of crime. Would I be tempted? Would my jail time limit my other choices so severely that I would take the easy route followed by so many when they walk out? I honestly couldn't be sure. I'd told Charlie and Ken:

Can't wait to walk out of these gates and hopefully never come back. I'll probably be up there diving on the reef before you know it, the thing is getting a job and if you could maybe try and line us up a job or something. I also have 12 months parole to do, I'll have to find out the do's and don'ts of that before I go romping around. I wouldn't mind just cruising around for a while, as I said before. I don't know what to do, I think I am going stir fucking crazy.

The night before my freedom, I didn't sleep at all, feeling more frightened and uncertain than I did the night before I walked in. I'd done my time, taken my punishment, and I'd survived it. I'd done more than that, too. I felt like a different person, one who knew things about myself and about the world that would change me forever. I'd been *happy* inside, developed bonds and understandings, and found a place where I felt safer and more certain than I'd ever been before. Whatever was on the other side, I was sure it wasn't that.

Mum, Dad, Sally and Leah were waiting for me at the gate, and Mum cuddled me and told me how exciting it was to be taking me home. I couldn't tell her that all I wanted to do at that moment was turn around and walk back inside.

Chapter 8

FREEDOM WAS not supposed to feel like this: out of jail, but wanting only to escape.

Cooranbong loomed as a new prison, one where I'd be watched and judged and despised, a place where I no longer knew the rules because there were different rules for someone like me. In a town so small that a stolen bicycle made the crime listings in the local paper, everyone knew what I'd done. Many people knew Adam Gosden and his family. And now I was an ex-con. I hadn't got a tattoo done in prison – a boob-tatt, as they were known in prison slang. Sam and Jim stopped me, adamant they wouldn't let me give myself a brand for life – but in Cooranbong I felt I had one anyway.

My first night outside, I wanted to see the ocean. I called Leigh Maule and asked her to take me for a drive. Of everyone I knew, she was the person I felt most comfortable with when I was down or confused, and that night I was both.

We drove north to Newcastle and sat on a beach and talked. The sound of the ocean was calming; other noises, the racket of the real world, jolted me, or sometimes gave me nervous reminders of where I'd come from. The rattle of keys, for instance, gave me the jitters; I tensed up at the barrage of traffic noise.

Later that week, a few old mates insisted I come for a beer at the local pub, which was a spit from where the accident happened. I had a drink, then walked outside alone to the car park and started pacing. That was how you did your thinking in prison, walking backwards and forwards, lost in your own mind, a daily routine. I hadn't been there long, but I had the habit. All I could think was that I had to be somewhere else. I couldn't be at this pub, where I imagined everyone was looking at me and passing judgement. *The killer drunk-driver with a beer in his hand.* I couldn't be with these people, my friends. They didn't understand me at all any more. I could feel the eyes in the back of my head. I paced and paced, then left the pub and went home.

I wanted nothing more than to head straight to Cairns to join Charlie and Ken, but I had no money, so that would have to wait. Dad was still working in Sydney, and got me a job in a scaffolding yard in Redfern. It was not the escape I had in mind, but it was something – I earned money, and spent every week in the city staying in Crows Nest. Dad and I shared a room. Every day I'd wake at dawn to catch the train from the North Shore to Redfern, where I'd work in the yard all day stacking scaffolding as it was returned from this or that building site. It was hard physical labour, the pay was dreadful, and at night I'd return to sleep in a cramped room with two single beds in it. The similarities to where I'd just come from didn't escape me, and in a way they were comforting. Dad was not inclined to press me to talk, and I didn't want to be pressed. For weeks, I spoke only when I needed to. As had been the case for years, the serious conversations raged only in my head.

On weekends, we'd head back to Cooranbong, where I did my best to keep out of sight. The only pleasure in those early days was being reunited with the horses, and I'd ride Buddy every weekend. While everyone around me wondered how I was and what prison was like and what I was going to do next, only my horse knew what I was thinking and feeling. Buddy knew I was going to disappear for as long as I could. He was the only one I really didn't want to leave behind.

I spoke to Ken and Charlie by phone.

We've got a place, Sutto, Ken said. *Come up here.*

Ken was a young journeyman, a jack of all trades. At that stage I was a jack of almost none, but Ken was sure I would find a job doing something. Cairns was like that, a tourist town, a stepping off point to other places, and I needed to step off to somewhere. So I bought a train ticket north, a ticket that would put 2000 kilometres between me and the past. I could be no one, or at least be someone else. I was running away, but I was running *to* something, too. I just didn't have a clue yet what it might be.

Dad drove me to Central Station in Sydney and we said goodbye on the platform. I could tell he was struggling with yet another goodbye.

When are we going to see you next?

I'll be back in a month.

I knew that was almost surely a lie, and I think he did, too. I walked away, then turned back to wave and knew he was fighting to hold back tears. How many times would I make him cry?

The train shot north, and in a feeling that would become familiar over the next few years I gave thanks that I lived in a land that offered me so much room for escape. A Parisian travelling that distance could have reached Russia; a Londoner would have made it to Turkey; a New Yorker would have landed in Havana. I arrived in Cairns, leaving half a continent behind me.

IT WAS hot, as it always is, hot enough to feel like another country, because even though it was the middle of winter, the skies were a pristine blue and the sun shone without the city regarding it as a surprise. Everyone wore shorts and T-shirts and thongs. Winter was for other places. Charlie and Ken met me at the station and took me home, such as it was – they were renting only a room, and I wouldn't be able to stay long. I didn't want to anyway. The point was to be alone; all I needed was a pit-stop while I worked out how to do it. Almost anything would do. I bought the *Cairns Post* and scanned the employment ads, finding what I wanted with ridiculous ease: an island resort in the middle of the Great Barrier Reef. They needed labourers to dig trenches, and to me it could not have sounded more perfect: all I needed to be able to do was dig a hole. In return, they'd accommodate me on a small, near-empty island in the middle of the Coral Sea. I'd have done it for nothing if necessary, but they hired me and signed me up at $700 a week, eight weeks on the island, two weeks off. Two days later, I was on a plane flying north to the place I wanted to be – a place that felt like nowhere.

The island was just 10 square kilometres of granite, surrounded by coral. Captain Cook found the island in 1770, and climbed to its peak to chart a course through the dangerous reefs around it. *The only land Animals we saw here were Lizards, and these seem'd to be pretty Plenty, which occasioned my naming the Island Lizard Island,* he wrote, and that's what it became. World famous now as an expensive resort, it had been something else for thousands of years. To the local Aboriginal people, it was Jiigurru, a sacred place used for initiating young men into the tribe and as a rich source of food from the sea. It had a place in the Dreamtime, and to the Dingaal people it was not a lizard but a stingray, with nearby islands forming its tail.

The resort was temporarily closed; we'd been hired to work on the renovations, digging trenches for electricity cables to power the lavish facilities that attracted travellers who ranged from tycoons with billions of dollars to pop stars who merely had millions. We, the labourers, slept in dongas – temporary aluminium sheds – and worked seven days a week, with a half-day's rest on Sunday. None of that mattered to me. Landing on Lizard was as liberating a moment as I'd had. I was further away from home and my messy past than I'd thought possible just a few weeks before, and when people asked who I was, I could sketch myself as large or small as I desired. These weren't people who wanted or needed to know much about you, and I was not keen on sharing. For the time being, I was content to draw a man just in outline, who took up as little room as possible.

All I had to do was dig holes, but there are holes, and then there are holes. These were *holes*. I was disbelieving when the foreman first told us just how long, wide, deep and complicated these trenches had to be, burrowing under roads and buildings, and dug largely by hand; it was too difficult to transport masses of earth-moving equipment from the mainland, and everything had to be done with care because, while it was a resort, Lizard Island was also a national park whose natural splendours protected it from over-development. As had happened with my recent work in Sydney, there was enough in the days to remind me of prison – the daily routine, the shared and rudimentary living quarters. There were dozens of us involved in the project, but I worked largely alone, setting targets in my head for how far I could dig each day.

We worked from early in the morning and through the heat of the day, the relief being that it was winter and therefore comfortably hot rather than unbearably humid. After the intensive fitness routine Sam and I had followed in jail and the weeks of hard labour in Sydney, I was up to the challenge. Physically, my body was tight as a drum. Mentally, I hadn't felt as light in years.

I spent a lot of my free time with the islanders working on the project, men from the Torres Straits, Fiji and New Caledonia, who were much more at home in the island setting than we white fellas. I did as I'd done in prison, falling in quickly with a new group of men who became my guides. The difference here was that I was learning how to enjoy the freedom that comes from immersing yourself in nature. They were physically impressive, and physically very different – at times I'd wonder at their affinity for the water, at their extraordinary understanding of what lived in and around it, and at how sometimes they seemed almost as one with it. Their skin glistened, and when they shook their heads the drops would fly off and they'd be instantly dry again. It didn't just *seem* as if they had been born to it; in many ways they had. These waters had been a source of life for millennia, and were still.

I'd swim and dive with the islanders, learning about the

sea life, what you could eat and what you couldn't, what to catch and how, then how to cook it. Green turtles – giant creatures the size of a small car – lived in the waters, and I learned how to hold on and be taken for a ride through the waves. There was a time, my new friends told me, when a green turtle would have been dinner for them, but now the species was endangered and protected. In any case, I was happier just to swim with them.

It was the first time I'd ever really found myself living side by side with people from a culture totally foreign to the Western one I was used to, and I felt comfortable and at home. As had always been the case, the natural world fulfilled me in a way nothing else could, and I had an unquenchable thirst for the kind of knowledge these men possessed – things I could never learn in a classroom.

The islanders accepted me openly and easily, and I them, and I knew it didn't sit comfortably with many of the other white men working on the island, who largely shunned the black workers.

The weeks passed almost without incident. I was barely communicating with the outside world, which is exactly how I wanted it, and slowly my head began to clear of the fears that had gripped me when I'd left jail. I knew Lizard Island was not a long-term solution, but it was the break I needed for me to see that this life on the other side of tragedy and prison might not be as hopeless as I'd thought it might be. If I could find this place and make a go of it, I could find others.

There was no plan beyond that, but it was enough to keep me moving forward. That's not to say I'd wiped the past from my mind. I thought every day of Adam Gosden and the letter I'd received from Arlea in jail. I still hadn't found the words or the courage to respond to it, but knew I would have to. If this journey was going to be worthwhile, that was going to have to be one of my destinations.

Another ghost came back to scare me, too. One night on the island, I was alone in a donga with one of the other workers. I had been drinking, and was lying down, half-asleep talking to him when I felt a hand on my leg. What he wanted was obvious so he didn't say anything, and he barely had time to utter a word anyway. I leapt up. *Jesus Christ, mate, what the fuck are you doing?*

As he said he was sorry, I fled, tormented as I'd always been that the thing I wanted was the thing that terrified me more than anything. Outside, I stopped to let my heart ease its pounding, and was dizzy from the electric charge that had shot through me when he touched me. I thought: *Go back in.* But I couldn't. The next morning, while we were working, he took me aside and apologised again. I told him it was okay and not to worry about it. I couldn't tell him how badly I'd wanted to respond in kind. No one knew me. No one would have known. I'd be moving on soon. But *I* would have known, and that was enough to stop me. We carried on working, and never mentioned it again.

When the eight weeks were up, they flew us back to the

mainland for our two-week break. I'd planned that I would return to the island when it was over, but that if something else came up that I wanted to do, I'd grab the opportunity. The key was not to allow myself time to get bored, and to keep myself as isolated as I could. I was revelling in being nobody.

We landed at Cairns airport and I went straight to a public phone to call Charlie and Ken. They didn't answer. On a whim, I went to the airport newsagency, bought the morning paper and turned to the job ads. It didn't take long. I knew where I was going next before I'd even left the terminal.

BLUEY MCGEE was in urgent need of a deckhand, and I thought I could convince him I was the man he needed. I called him from the airport and he told me to come straight over for an interview. I walked outside, got in a taxi and told the driver to take me to the wharf where the fishing trawlers were based, a place known as the Pig Pen. I found the right boat, and waiting for me on board was Bluey. He was a short but strong man in his fifties, and the red hair that had given him his nickname was in fast retreat. He looked like someone had just prised him off a rock on the ocean floor.

Bluey was, in his way, as much a part of the sea as the islanders I'd met on Lizard, but to him it was a business. He came from a long line of fishermen and had been on the water since he was a boy. Now he fished the waters north of the Australian mainland for prawns from the start of the season in March to the end in November, and halfway through the 1995 season he was a deckhand short. Had I worked on a boat before? Not exactly, I said, but I was completely at home on the water. Those days and nights with Dad on Sydney Harbour suddenly took on great importance, and I exaggerated my skills and experience a little to convince him I could do the job. We'd be at sea without a break for three months, he said. Just me, him, and another decky.

Reckon you can handle that?

Of course I could. I didn't tell him then, but they were the sweetest words I'd ever heard. The pay was terrible – five per cent of the earnings from the total catch, with the risk that through bad weather, bad luck or bad management, there might be days when we didn't catch much at all. And he'd take 10 dollars a day out of my pay for food, so theoretically there were days when I'd be earning nothing, or even paying him. In return, I'd have to work on the deck, cook and clean. There would be nowhere to go if I got to sea and found I hated it, but I didn't care. I'd have paid him to take me.

I'll give you a go. Be back here tomorrow morning. We're leaving at seven.

I left the wharf, booked a room for the night, then called Mum and Dad to tell them what I was doing. Too excited to sleep, I spent the hours between then and sunrise letting the coming adventure unfold in my mind. To many people, what I was about to do would have seemed an act of desperation, the kind of job you'd take as a last resort – isolated, dangerous, poorly paid. To me, it was the luckiest of breaks.

I headed back to the Pig Pen before seven and boarded my new home. Bluey was getting the *Krar* ready to move out, and the other decky, Mark, was there. He'd done prawn runs before and knew the ropes – literally, as I discovered, because one thing I knew nothing about was the sailor's art of ropes and knots. I needed to learn fast, but for the moment I couldn't do much more than watch.

As we motored out of the harbour, I was elated just to stand on the deck and take it all in. It was a long time since I'd had reason to feel proud, but that morning I did. It was less than 24 hours since I'd landed at Cairns airport, and now I was *here.* That was the greatest thrill, that I'd been brave and confident enough to let my life turn in a moment, and to embrace the uncertainty and opportunity rather than hide from it. Dazzled by my own achievement, I was just as awed by the beauty of the day and the spectacle of the sea that carried us.

The water changed colour as we moved out, from grey to blue to green. In parts it was perfectly clear and you could see the sea life coursing beneath us. I wanted to see everything, and to know everything. I couldn't sit still. Bluey was in the wheelhouse navigating, wearing the ship's uniform – a singlet and underpants. He had his bare feet up on the wheel, and I think was eyeing me with a kind of weary indulgence. He'd seen them young, green and mad keen before, and he'd see young blokes like me again. All the old salt had to do was harness the spirit.

It was going to take three days to reach the Torres Straits, so I had time to learn at least some of what I'd need to know to survive 100 days at sea. With only three of us on board, we all had to be able to navigate so we could take turns at the wheel while the others slept. It was intimidating, but not as hard as it sounded. The *Krar* was fitted with a global positioning system device, and that first afternoon I had a crash course in how to guide the boat precisely where we wanted it to go, plotting our route on the GPS, which was even able to take the boat on a safe course through coral reefs that would once have demanded an extraordinary eye, steady hands and a steely mind to navigate.

Bluey had Mark teach me about ropes and knots, what needed to be tied where, and how, and when. That first day and night, I refused to sleep – and couldn't have slept if I'd tried. I passed the hours learning from Mark, or at Bluey's side in the wheelhouse. After dark on the first night, he sent me into the galley to cook dinner. We were each to cook a meal a day, and that was one task I could take to with confidence: I'd become a resourceful chef in prison, so much so that after he left, Sam would write letters saying how much he missed my cook-ups. On the *Krar*, supplies were plentiful and I honed that useful skill, turning out a decent meal using one small hot plate, a couple of pans and whatever food I had in front of me at the time. We ate, and eventually Bluey ordered me to get some rest.

You're driving next. I'll be going to bed.

Bluey was giving me the wheel after less than 24 hours at sea. I doubt he slept a wink, but he had the faith to give me a go and the wisdom to realise that if I was going to be of any use I'd have to develop the skills and confidence quickly. Alone in the wheelhouse, I was terrified and exhilarated – the captain of the ship. I sat back and put my feet up, like Bluey did. I plotted our course on the GPS, taking us slightly off line at times as I got used to the small delay between what the boat was doing and what the satellite system was showing me. But I guided us north for hours without mishap, and as someone inclined to think in simple metaphors, I felt like I was steering myself in the right direction at last.

BY DAY four Bluey and Mark had taught me as much as they could, but nothing can prepare you for the bedlam and intensity of your first night on deck – when the boards shoot away from the end of the booms on either side of the boat and the nets drop to the bottom of the ocean, trawling for prawns. It's only done at night, starting at sunset, and the work day doesn't end till long after sunrise. On some boats the skipper would leave the gritty end of the catch work to the deckies, but Bluey would put the boat on auto-pilot and do the hard work with us, putting his head into the wheelhouse every now and then to check we were on course and that there were no dangers looming. The try-net would come up and down every 20 minutes, literally testing the waters to give us an idea of the size and quality of the catch being scooped into the giant nets below. When the net came up, we'd line it up over the giant sorting tray on the deck and let her go – the haul would crash and scatter onto the boat.

We caught thousands and thousands of prawns, but also more than that. You can't send giant nets to the ocean floor without snaring thousands of other creatures along with the targets, and the deck could be turned into a wet and bloody mass of sea life, great and small – from sharks and giant stingrays to deadly sea snakes and catfish with spikes that could rip your hands apart. It's dark, working under floodlights and the moon, with no noise other than the sounds of thrashing fish and shouts across the deck as the real work of the evening begins. There is not a second of down time. Everything that's been dumped on the deck has to be sorted, the prawns separated into breed and size and the unwanted stuff thrown back.

The night of my first catch I was slow but charged by the sheer excitement of the moment. I got down on the deck and plunged my bare hands into the chaos in front of me. I'd cast an occasional glance over to Bluey and Mark, who'd done it all before. They could fill a bucket with prawns in the time it took me to have one a quarter full. We each had a bucket for endeavours, tigers and kings, and another one for what were called smash-and-dash – the useless broken ones. Then they had to be sorted according to weight and price – or as good a guess as you could make there on the deck. The smallest prawns would go into the 30-plus bucket – meaning it would take at least 30 of them to make a pound; the larger ones were called the under-tens, because you'd need only that many to make weight. Bluey had told me to wear gloves for the first few nights, but I didn't listen as he wasn't wearing any, and Mark wasn't either. My paws were soon bloodied and raw, immersed for hours in the saltwater and ripped by the spikes and sharp edges that met my hands every time I grabbed a fresh pile from the sorting tray.

The night didn't end with the sorting of the catch. The prawns had to be boxed and stored, the deck cleaned, the nets examined and repaired. It was well after sunrise before we could rest. After my first night on the catch, I was exhausted and sore, but deliriously happy. I'd at last lived a day that would send me to bed certain of sleeping peacefully. It had been a long time since that had happened.

So started my year at sea. Not all of it would be quite as tranquil.

Chapter 9

AM I going to bleed to death?

The question was mine. The answer came from Bluey.

Fish bleed a lot.

He was trying to calm me down by making me think most of the blood I could see flooding over the deck came from the haul of the night before, but I knew from a glance at the gushing hole in my left arm that enough of it was coming from me to have him worried.

Bluey didn't worry much about anything, at least not that he let on, but this was making him nervous. We were in the middle of the ocean, with no hope of a quick rescue. All we could try to do was staunch the flow and hope for the best. The gushing wouldn't stop, though, and I was too panicked at first to do what I needed to: keep the large absorbent pad he'd grabbed from the first-aid kit pressed tightly to the wound. I couldn't stop pulling the pad away, to see if the flood was easing. But I'd cut into a vein and was painting the deck an ever deeper, thicker red, amazed that a small hole in my arm could let loose this torrent. I was being drained of blood and sapped of strength.

Bluey shouted at me: *Keep the pad tight. Stop pulling the fucking thing off.*

But he was not as angry as he might have been, given that as ever I'd brought the disaster on myself. We'd finished work for the night and I had been ready to settle in to what had become my morning routine of fishing off the boat once the prawn catch had been sorted. I spotted some tuna at the rear of the *Krar* and remembered Bluey's stories about the money to be made from them. His rule was that any fish I caught independently of the main catch was mine to sell, and as the weeks went by I built up a healthy stock that would bring me a few hundred extra dollars. What I'd never done until that morning was pole a tuna, but I'd heard Bluey talk about it and saw my chance to snare a decent pile of cash.

I grabbed a metal pole and attached a broken fish hook to the end, giving me a makeshift spear. It should never have worked, but it did and before long I had four large tuna on the deck. I'd swing the pole into the swell behind the boat, and rip it back quickly over the boat, bringing the tuna with it. Then the pole snapped. The bent hook came off and ripped back into my forearm, scoring a direct hit with the vein.

Hearing me yell, Bluey ran out into the stream of blood. *What the fuck have you done?*

He was at least impressed by the tuna.

It wasn't the first or last time during my days at sea that I thought I might die. Bluey was not inclined to fuss; a degree of danger went with the territory, and if you didn't like it then you shouldn't be there. Naturally reckless and most alive when taking risks, I agreed with his philosophy and tried never to sulk or complain or shy from a moment of fear. Being as isolated as we were, we lived or died according to our own wits and ability, because help was always a long way away.

That day, the day I asked him if I was going to die on his deck with blood streaming from my arm, the only means of rescue was an emergency call on the radio to summon a helicopter. It would have cost a small fortune, and taken so long that it might have been useless anyway. So we took a punt that if I could stem the flow for long enough it would eventually stop before my heart did. It worked, and I was back on deck sorting prawns the next morning.

I ENDED up doing four trips over two seasons, taking a different third crewman each time. Mark, the head decky on my first trip, didn't make it to the end of the run. He'd woken one night with his body jerking, thrashing around and cracking his head against the bunk above him. The fit frightened Bluey more than anything I ever saw, and neither of us knew what to do to help him. Bluey had no idea what was happening; I'd seen an epileptic seizure before and could only assume that was what it was. When Mark stopped moving and fell back on his bed asleep, we checked his pulse and tended his wound, then left him to rest. We didn't know what else to do. He slept for most of the next day, while Bluey stormed around, angry that Mark hadn't told him about his epilepsy, and worried what would happen if he had a seizure at the wrong moment. What if he fell overboard?

Bluey decided he had to let Mark go, so we dropped him off when we next met with the supply vessel known as the mother ship, which kept the trawlers stocked with food and other supplies. I was now Bluey's senior, and only, decky. For the last three weeks of that trip, we were two up – Bluey and me.

Bluey became a mentor and father-figure. He told me about his life, growing up in Port Lincoln in South Australia, where his father and grandfather had been tuna fishermen, and unfurled his own stories of life on the sea. And I told him about my past, or as much of it as I could bear to part with. It still wasn't much, but I eventually found the balls to tell him about the accident, and that I'd been in prison.

Bluey absorbed the news without blinking. It was hard to surprise him, but I didn't want to push my luck by telling him my other secret, and I had pushed it so far down

I didn't often think about it. I'd found a life I could live, without worrying about whether I was gay or not, whether I would marry and have kids, what my family would think. By the end of that first trip, I thought I knew what I wanted to do: own a trawler, spend most of my life alone at sea, never worry about what happened in the real world or have the real world worry about me. Bluey proved it could be done. He was my new hero, and I had complete faith in him, even when defiance might have been a wiser course.

On one trip, the junior decky Bluey had hired forgot to tie one edge of a net properly and it came loose and fell back into the sea. It got caught in the propeller, putting not just the rest of the trip at risk but leaving the boat in danger of seizing completely. Bluey, furious, saw only one solution: I was going to have to dive under the boat and cut the net loose.

It was night, and I knew as well as Bluey did that there were sharks nearby. There always were. They were there day and night, following the boat, often getting caught in the nets themselves and ending up thrashing about on the deck. I was used to dealing with sharks on deck; I wasn't used to swimming with them at night while trying to repair a propeller with a net caught in its blades. My head told me to say no, but I couldn't get the word out. I would go in.

I put the air tank on, grabbed a torch and jumped over, adding another entry to the expanding ledger listing the moments I thought I might be about to die. The mess below was worse than we'd thought and I returned to the surface to tell Bluey I'd need tools and time to fix it. Then I pointed at Tony, the decky, and shouted at him, *You're fucking coming with me!*

Smarter than I was, Tony refused at first but could see I'd probably force him in if he didn't come voluntarily. *It's your fucking fault,* I told him. And besides, there was no way I could do the repair job without someone holding a torch. Over we went. We were down there for 45 minutes, but the sharks left us alone. I think it was that night that Bluey realised there was nothing I wouldn't do for him, and that he could trust me with anything.

I loved the danger, wherever it came from. If a giant stingray the size of a backyard trampoline landed on the deck when we dropped the catch, I'd be ready to jump in and help the skipper get it off again. Bluey would lift the ray's enormous head off the deck with a pole, and I'd then feed a rope through its mouth and out through its gills. Then we'd pull the rope out to one of the booms that swept out from the side of the boat. To get the ray back in the water, I'd have to climb out and sit on the edge of the boom and push it up, lifting the ray off the deck, then swing the boom out away from the boat and cut it loose. Sitting on the boom, with only the ocean underneath me, Bluey didn't need to tell me the obvious truth. It was the middle of the catch, when sharks swarm around the boat. *If I fall in, I'm fucked.*

I had no special skills that enabled me to survive, just

the blend of confidence and recklessness that subdues fear. If I was in control, I was always okay. When I wasn't in control, as when I rode out two cyclones on the *Krar*, I was more jittery but learned from example.

The first cyclone was as terrifying as anything else I'd encountered. When it's nature giving you the trouble, there's only so much you can do to stop her. That first time, Bluey was calm as the waves crashed over the boat and everything that hadn't been tied down was thrown loose, including me. He told me to relax – that it was only the tail-end of the storm and that we'd be okay. The second time, I was calm, because by then we had another new decky and I was determined to paint a picture of nonchalant experience, just like Bluey.

Nothing to worry about, mate, I told the new bloke. *We'll be fine.*

We always were, and the scars left from these occasional disasters were only physical. Other than my attachment to Bluey, I didn't need to lead any sort of emotional life at sea. That was fine with me. The deeper I could bury it, the better. Human problems intruded only once, on my third trip on the *Krar* when Bluey had to return to the mainland to deal with a family crisis. We got a replacement skipper, a man I knew only as Knuckles, and after months of getting used to Bluey's ways and rules I was unhappy to learn there were other ways of running a boat. Knuckles may have been left in charge, but I believed Bluey was relying on me to look after his boat and his catch. Knuckles ran a looser ship – we worked less, drank more, called in to islands we'd once have passed by so he could stock up on his dope supply. Once I saw him pay for it with part of the catch – Bluey's catch. *My* catch. Things were slipping.

One day, Knuckles' carelessness forced me back into waters teeming with sharks after the dinghy we used to get between shore and our boat came loose and drifted away. The only way to get it back was to dive in and swim after it, and I nearly expired trying. I got the dinghy, returned to the *Krar* and briefly contemplated tossing the old bastard overboard. Instead, I contacted Bluey using the boat radio and told him things were falling apart. If Knuckles was going to stay, I was leaving. He was angry to hear how poorly his replacement was running things, but calmed me down and told me he'd be back to the *Krar* before long. I let Knuckles live.

I COULDN'T abandon life on land entirely. The prawn runs went for three months and after each trip all the trawlers would return to Cairns and eject crews of men who were by then as hungry for a party as a navy man on shore leave. I'd managed to track down Ken again, who by then had broken up with Charlie and taken up with Lynne Chassion, a Canadian traveller. Lynne and I bonded quickly, finding from the start that we could talk easily and openly. I'd also see Charlie, who had stayed on in Cairns and was working at a popular backpacker bar, and I stumbled across two other old school mates who had travelled north like me and found work on the boats. It almost felt like home – familiar faces, shared histories, companionship and support.

My second trip with Bluey was aborted after just a week at sea because of a problem with the navigation system, so when we unexpectedly returned to shore to repair it I found myself back in Cairns in time to celebrate my 21st birthday.

We ended up late that night at Johnno's Blues Bar, a Cairns institution. Ken and Lynne eventually surrendered to tiredness and went home, leaving me sitting at the bar alone, drinking. The stool next to mine was empty, and a young bloke walked in and sat down next to me, brushing his knee against my leg. We started talking and he bought me a drink. An hour passed before he said he was leaving. Did I want to come for a walk? I said yes. We left the bar and started walking and soon enough he said he lived nearby. Why didn't I come there for a last drink? I agreed.

We got to his flat and I sat on the couch. Then he came over, stood in front of me, leaned over and put his hands on my knees. He leaned in and tried to kiss me, but I pulled back. He jerked back upright, surprised.

You haven't done this much before, have you?

No, I said.

But this time I wasn't going to run away. He tried again,

and this time I responded. I kissed him back. Suddenly it was as if he had flicked a switch, and years of denial and confusion and hatred washed away as I gave in and just let it happen. God knows what he thought, because once I'd started I didn't want to stop. I stayed with him all night and kept him awake for most of it. I left in the morning to return to the boat. We were due to head out to sea again later that day.

I thought about him for days, reliving what had happened. My mood swung from elation to disgust that I had done it again, and enjoyed it so much. It was the first time that I'd felt completely sexually alive. I knew that if I hadn't had to leave for the boat I would have been back to see him the next night, the next and the next. But as had happened after the encounter in high school, revulsion was on hand to temper the joy of discovery. I still hated myself for even thinking or dreaming about it, so actually doing it inspired moments of deep self-loathing. The battle inside, trying to reconcile pleasure with what I thought was perversion, carried on without resolution. I couldn't have a sensible conversation about it with myself, and remained too terrified to discuss it honestly with anyone else. In the end, I told a stranger.

Earlier that year, Australian rugby league star Ian Roberts had come out, an event that drew huge publicity because he was the first Australian sports star to tell the world he was gay. It was a small turning point for me, too, because he was the first well-known gay man I knew something about, and could in some way identify with. He shattered the stereotype: a muscle-bound man-mountain who was feared and admired for his abilities in a field that made no allowance for sissies. Knowing he was gay somehow made it seem more okay that I might be, too.

Out on the boat, with my head spinning after the encounter on my 21st, I made a small but crucial step forward towards acceptance. I wrote Ian Roberts a letter. It was the first time I had actually shared the words *I think I might be gay* with anyone, and it says a lot for how alone and confused I was that it happened in a letter to a stranger. But the experience was cathartic: once I started writing, I couldn't stop, and so it was that a sporting celebrity I had never met became the first person on the planet to hear the truth about the real me. I told him that I had these feelings and thoughts and that I didn't know how to handle them. I didn't know how to tell anyone. I didn't know what to do or where to go, or know how to find a way to live with it. I poured everything into that letter, put it in an envelope and addressed it to:

Ian Roberts
C/- Manly-Warringah Rugby League Club
Sydney, NSW.

I have no idea if he ever received it. He never replied, but it didn't matter. The act of committing the words to paper and passing them to another human being was a big enough breakthrough for me. But telling a stranger was one thing. To those who knew me, I would still try to explain away the reasons I'd never had a girlfriend – that I was the type of guy who didn't like to answer to anybody else, that having a girlfriend would just complicate my life. I'd write often to Lynne, Ken's Canadian girlfriend. She was one of the few people who asked openly about my personal life. Writing back, I'd add to her confusion, and my own.

Maybe I need love in my life, who knows? I've just been the type of guy that loves my own little life, having to not really answer to anybody or worry too much. I don't think I need it yet, but I think I probably would, well, how would you say it, ummm – fall in love easily. I'll just take things as they come, if it happens it happens. Answers never come easily, do they? I get all anxious all the time, wondering what I want to do in life, what I will be and if everything will be all right.

In another letter, I wrote:

You are asking how I am still going seven years or whatever it is without a girlfriend. There's been no shortage of offers, but I don't know. I am just happy the way things are going and having a girlfriend might complicate things. Plus, I wouldn't know where to start. It's a bit embarrassing, eh? There's been rumours going around at home that I am gay, cause I never went out and rooted around.

People are funny how they judge people for not doing some things. Everyone says that all guys think with their dicks, and sex is everything. Sure, sex is good, but it's not something I have to have every week and I can go without it for ages and not be worried by it. I know I carry on like a kid sometimes, maybe I think it's cause the thought of growing up scares me a bit. It's not going to be all fun and games in the real world.

I WAS scared, that much is clear reading back over my words now. The encounter on my 21st had left me emotionally wrung out. Other evenings in Cairns, the damage was physical. Those shore breaks marked the first time since the accident that I'd had much to drink, and I found myself getting drunk too quickly. Trouble came with it.

One night I woke up on the street, covered in blood and with my face beaten to a pulp. One of my front teeth had been knocked backwards and now sat horizontally, pointing to the back of my mouth. My right eye was swollen and dried shut with caked blood, and my body was cut and bruised. I had no idea what had happened to me, or how I'd ended up there, only that I'd been out with friends to a bar the night before. When I came to, I was being put on a stretcher and carted to an ambulance. I passed out again and regained consciousness in hospital, sitting in a wheelchair. I was due to sail with Bluey that afternoon.

They patched me up, then sent me to a dentist to have the tooth examined. He pretended to be just having a close look at it. Then, without warning, he gripped it between two fingers and yanked it back into position. The pain was excruciating, but he said there was little else he could do.

With an agonising mouth injury, an eye I couldn't see out of, and cuts and bruises from top to toe, I headed straight down to the wharf. I'd missed the scheduled departure, but Bluey was waiting and, as I approached the boat, the crews on other trawlers took one look at me and broke into a chorus of catcalls and applause. Bluey appeared on the deck and looked down.

You're fucking lucky you turned up looking like that, he said. *Because if you hadn't, I'd have done the job for you.*

To this day, I have no idea what happened. Had I been so drunk that I hit on a man, and got poofter-bashed for my trouble? It seemed possible, but it was a total blank then, and it's an even darker hole in my memory now. I hadn't been robbed, just beaten, and my friends could only tell me that they'd lost track of me in the pub and hadn't seen me again until I turned up in hospital. There were no signs that I'd fought back; my own fists had not been used. Whatever had happened, one thing was clear: whether I was to blame or not, it was alcohol again that had landed me in trouble. I'd used it in the past, and would again in the future, to ease pain, to black things out, to stop me from thinking, to transform myself into a different, happier man. But I could also go for long periods drinking little or not at all; then I'd be careless. For the second time in my life, it was the cause of real physical and emotional pain. I was a long time learning how useless a security blanket alcohol is.

As I got back on the boat that afternoon, one eye barely open and hardly able to speak, I was just relieved I still had a job. Bluey didn't say much more. We set sail again the next morning, one day late.

BACK IN Cooranbong, my family heard sporadically about my adventures and disasters. I could send and receive mail only once or twice a month, because all letters had to be sent via the ships' agent in Cairns, then delivered via the mother ship. We'd meet up with it about once a fortnight to stock up on food, fresh water and anything else we needed, to hand over the mail we wanted posted and to collect anything that had been sent to us. Mum and Dad had less of an idea what I was doing while at sea than they did while I was in prison, but I think at least they sensed I was happier than I'd been in a long time. During one of my longer shore breaks, the whole family – Mum, Dad, Sally and Leah – came to Cairns and we had a family holiday, our first in many years. That helped put their minds at rest. I was as tanned, healthy and fit as it was possible to be, and they could see I was thriving.

Over the long, end-of-season break in December that year, with three months before the prawn season started again, I flew home. I got a short-term job at the marina in Newcastle, and Mum and Dad threw me a belated 21st with the home crowd. Friends and relatives turned up by the dozen to celebrate. I felt more comfortable being back than I had after jail, but still knew I was not ready to come home for good.

As happy as I was, everything is relative and I was only comparing my frame of mind to the misery that had gripped me before. The memories still wouldn't leave me. There wasn't a day that Adam Gosden didn't come to mind, and I was slowly realising that he and I would live quietly together forever. What I had done to him in some ways now defined me, if not to the outside world then certainly to me. Some of it was guilt. Some of it was a feeling that I had to redeem myself in his eyes. Some of it was the knowledge that I had been given a second chance, and I had to embrace it on his behalf as much as mine. I'd be doing him no favours by wasting my life, after already wasting his.

The morning of the second anniversary of the accident I went into the garden at home and gathered some flowers. Someone had told me Adam was buried at Morisset cemetery, so I drove there alone and walked from one end of it to the other, searching for his grave. There were nearly 2000 of them, and I couldn't find one for Adam. I'd been told the wrong place, I realised, but I went and sat alone on a bench anyway and talked to him, sometimes out loud and sometimes in my head, and told him again that I was sorry for what I'd done. I was crying. I was trying to find some way to say goodbye to someone I'd never met, and to seek their forgiveness and understanding, a kind of grief and guilt for which there is no guide.

In February, I returned to Cairns to rejoin Bluey for the start of the new season. Once at sea, I knew I could do what I'd needed to do for two years. I sat down one night while Bluey slept and found a moment of perfect calm in the darkness, surrounded by water and an unexpected peace. I started writing.

Dear Arlea,
I have wanted to write to you now for quite some time. I know that I have really wanted to, but never knew how it would be accepted. After receiving your letter it put me at ease writing one in return. I am sorry for this one's extreme delay as well, at the moment I am in the middle of the waters of the Torres Strait on a prawn trawler.

My life was changed and so was yours on that tragic day, it's something I really don't try to remember too quickly. We've both been through a hell of a lot, you so much more, losing a part of your family. You seem to be a very strong person. Arlea, I really didn't know how I was going to cope. I was a complete mess. My life fell apart around me. I lost a grip on myself. I started counselling which slowly helped me put myself and my life back into place. I turned myself away from family and friends for a while, only wanting to sulk in my own misery. If it wasn't for me doing counselling, I am not sure whether or not I would still be here today.

I know a lot of rumours spread about the accident, as rumours do. I really just want you to know that I'm sorry with all my heart, body and soul and that if there is anything I can ever do for you, I will. Nothing will ever bring your brother Adam back except lovely memories that you hold. At least we know that he has gone to the gates of eternal life, a place in Heaven, and may God look well after him. Also, I want you to know that I am not some drunken lout and it's not something I've done before or will be ever doing again. It was an extremely hard way to learn a lesson.

Adam

I wrote a draft first, scribbling out mistakes, then copied it out again neatly for posting. I wondered if she'd ever reply. I knew as I wrote it that it didn't matter. I'd taken a small step towards joining a broken circle.

Just stay away, mate. He's gone.

And may God look well after him.

I'd never been religious, had hardly ever been to church, but Mum was a woman of strong faith who sometimes spoke in sacred terms, offering prayer in troubled times and seeking guidance from a higher authority. After the accident she had written to Adam's mother. Mum had learned that she was also a religious woman, and so wrote a letter of condolence and regret. It was, as she described it, a letter from one mother to another, and one Christian to another. Adam, I learned much later, was also a man who drew comfort from his faith. He would go to church and take confession. I could claim no such relationship with God. But I could find solace in the language, and comfort in the belief that there might be understanding and redemption somewhere beyond ourselves. It seemed right to draw on those words as I struggled to express myself in the hardest letter I would ever write.

I sealed it. Then, alone in the dark on the deck, I cried again.

THAT WAS my last trip with Bluey, and it was a long one – four months at sea, just the two of us, and by the end of it I think we both knew it was time for me to move on. We'd never had a serious disagreement about anything, but by the time it was over we'd spent a total of a year together in confined quarters. Relationships formed under such intense circumstances run their course, or at least require a break. When we got back to Cairns, we said goodbye – a handshake, and an understanding that I could come back when I wanted to. He'd been one of the giant men in my life, in some ways a saviour, even though he didn't know it himself. I'd found my pride, something I'd never possessed in abundance, and rediscovered my joy for life.

Prison had made me a man, but I'd come out not knowing what sort of a man I was. For all the doubts inside, life with Bluey had shown me that I could become a good one.

Chapter 10

BUT WHERE to next? Ken Rockley again had the answer. He'd left Cairns for good by the time I finished my last trip with Bluey and crossed the continent to Broome, on the opposite side of the country. I flew home first to spend some time with Mum and Dad, then called Ken in the west. As he'd done two years before, he gave me the only nudge I needed. *Come over, mate. We'll find you some work.* I didn't stop to think about it.

Broome was the better part of 5000 kilometres away, two-and-a-half times as far from home as Cairns had been, and again the distance was liberating. So was Broome itself. The locals have a word – *Broometime* – to describe the way of life and state of mind. Things happen as they happen. It's a place of heat and beauty, perched on the north-west coast between a sea so blue you could weep and a rich red desert. In its colours and heat, it is like another world again, a place where you could go to the edge of town and see dinosaur footprints in the rocks by the sea. In modern times it was a frontier town, with a history pocked by tragedy and triumph – from the settlement wars with the Aboriginals, to the boom years in the late 1800s when it became a pearling mecca after the discovery of the world's largest pearl shell. Broome nearly died during World War II, when the Japanese bombed Roebuck Bay and the townspeople fled in fear of invasion. The war ended and, though it took years to recover, the pearls saved the place, as they always did.

By the time I arrived in early 1998, Broome was undergoing a slow transformation: it had been discovered by tourists – rich ones who demanded luxury resorts, and the budget brigade who turned it into one of Australia's backpacking havens. But I went there not as a traveller; I wanted to stay and work. I knew there was a living to be made at sea.

I stayed with Ken for a few days. Lynne had returned to Canada by then and he lived in a house he shared with several women. A walk through scrub with a surfboard on my back and I was on Cable Beach, which seemed to stretch forever – and the house was big enough that they gave me my own room. It was an easy life to fall in love with: hot and slow and friendly. Then, out of nowhere, work appeared, just as it had when I first got to Cairns. Ken knew someone, who knew someone, who knew someone else who could get me a job. In short order, I was taken on by Broome Pearls, part of the giant Kailis group, one of the biggest companies farming the precious gems.

The interview wasn't difficult.

Have you ever spent three weeks on a boat?

Have I what. Three weeks, and then some.

It was casual labour that didn't demand any particular skill, just a willingness to work long days and to tolerate the time at sea. That obviously did not faze me; what did was the size of the boat and the number of people on board. It was harvest season and there were 35 crew on the largest vessel I'd ever been on. The dynamic was utterly different to the close-knit male camaraderie I'd experienced with Bluey on the trawler. On the pearling boat there were men and women, and a clear hierarchy. We – the short-term staff – were at the bottom of the ladder. We were brought on to work on the deck, clean shells in the operations room and get the shells to the technicians who seeded the oysters to produce the pearls.

I didn't enjoy the work, but the journey itself along the far north coast of Western Australia was spectacular. The sunsets were beyond description, and to me a new phenomenon: growing up on the east coast of Australia, I had never seen the sun set behind the ocean at day's end. After three weeks, we returned to Broome. I was asked to sign on for another trip, but I'd already decided this was not the job for me. I took my money, and put myself in Ken's hands again. I knew he'd always come up with something.

*

KEN WAS an electrician, and in Broome he had found a way to turn his trade into what would later become a lucrative and rewarding business. The far north-west was home to Aboriginal communities in areas so remote they presented unique challenges in the supply of basic services such as electricity. The power supply had to be installed, maintained, repaired and upgraded, and Ken was establishing himself as a key bidder for those government contracts. It was demanding and risky work, travelling sometimes for weeks at a time to parts of the country few white people ever visited. In this part of the country, you were always a long way from anywhere. Help could never come in a hurry if something went wrong. And cultural differences meant the people who went in there needed to go equipped with more than their practical skills.

Some communities had little time for white fellas, sometimes because they had experienced too little contact, in other cases because they had experienced too much. But Ken loved entering this other world, and invariably found a way to accept and to be accepted wherever he went. If his friendship was a blessing to me in those days, so was the opportunity he gave me to join him on his journeys to people and places that added a new layer to my understanding of the country I was born in.

I did half a dozen trips with him to Aboriginal communities. Sometimes we drove – and the trip out alone could take days – and we'd sleep in the back of a truck or camp out in our swags. Other times we went in small planes flown by pilots who had to be able to land anywhere. On one trip, the pilot had to start counting sand dunes from the air to know where he was supposed to land.

The landscapes could toy with your mind; at Balgo, I walked alone for an hour carrying my camera to what I was convinced was a water hole in the middle of the desert. I'd seen a mirage before, but never one as convincing as this. The closer I got to it, the more real it appeared. I can see it now even in the photos I took as I thumped through the sand. Ken had given me two pieces of advice as I set off on that fruitless walk: *There's nothing there, Sutto. I'm telling you, it's a mirage.* And: *Be back by sunset. We're being locked away for the night.*

He was right on both counts. We'd been told that alcohol was a major problem in that community, and that violence sometimes flared. So, in the middle of the outback, that endless space, we were locked in a small compound from sundown to sunrise, fenced in by wire. There was never a suggestion of aggression or trouble, but I was in no position to argue.

Weeks later, back in Broome, Ken took a call that signalled the start of the most memorable trip we would make together. Pantijan was exotic and rare even for these parts. Few white people had ever been there. In their tribal area in the remotest of places in the far north-west, isolation was a geographical fact for the Pantijan and probably an historical blessing, because it was a community largely untouched by the curses of alcoholism, petrol-sniffing, violence and disease that afflict some Aboriginal communities.

The only way for us to get in was by air, and we flew in on a small plane and were greeted by a small strip of land that ended abruptly in a small hill. That was the runway. The landing had to be precise. There were four of us on board – Ken, his sidekick Bruce, the pilot and me. I'd been brought along as the trade assistant and cook for the duration of the job.

A handful of children and a couple of men ran out to greet us and the pilot flew out again straight away; we had no way out again until he came back, which he said would be in about a week. We were there to fix the power supply, which ran off a generator that had broken down, but on first landing we wondered who we were fixing it for. There seemed to be hardly anyone there. An elder pointed us to a small shed on the side of the runway, which was a little power station. He was generous with his time, and greeted us warmly, making it clear we were welcome.

The next day, more people appeared, and then more, until it became apparent that the place was home to a large, thriving mob spanning four generations. There were children by the dozen, unhindered by suspicion of white men and unrestrained in their fascination with us. They hadn't seen many of us before. Many of them had never seen a city, or even a town as big as Broome, and the ocean was a mystery to them. In my memory, they showed us only smiles and joy. *Copy me*, they'd cry when they saw the camera, pleading with me to take their photograph.

One little girl attached herself to me on the second day and wouldn't let go, gripping my leg or climbing on my back to make sure she came with me everywhere I went. She didn't seem to understand anything I said, and it took a day for me to realise that she was all but completely deaf. But little during that week was communicated using words. Little was really being communicated at all. I wish I could say I came away with a deep understanding of the people we'd met. But it would have taken more time and far greater trust and understanding than we, or they, had then to even scratch the surface. I never fully understood the initiation ritual that left men with deep scars across their chests, or the meaning of their sacred sites – why they could take us to this lagoon, but not another.

It was the most magical of weeks. It's easy to sound trite and even sentimental talking about a people and a place like this, but I witnessed an indelible bond between people, land, water and sky in those few days. I can summon it in my memory today because it remains the only time I have ever sensed it. Instinctively, it demanded that we be totally respectful. It never seemed less than right that we should behave as visitors; we were all citizens of the same country, but there was not a doubt in my mind that the Pantijan belonged to something else, something deeper, than anything represented by my passport or birth certificate.

I WAS learning that if you're willing to do anything, anything is what you'll end up doing. You could call it desperation. I preferred to see it as making my own luck, and being open to experience. I didn't need comforts, and was usually happier without them – comfort and adventure rarely went hand in hand, and I'd long ago realised that adventure was what fired up my spirit. Back in Broome with time on my hands, it didn't take long for someone to strike a match.

Ken and I were in a pub one night and began a conversation with a bloke who was drinking alone. He asked me what I was doing in Broome. Not much right now, I told him. *Well,* he said, *I'm working out at a mine near Fitzroy Crossing. I know a bloke who needs workers. You interested?*

I was. My new mate, John, gave me the number for Alan Trotter and told me to call him, using his name as an introduction. I called the next day, and realised immediately that his surname was a misnomer. Alan never trotted. He did everything at a gallop, and that included talking. I told him who I was, and then struggled to get a word in edgeways.

Yeah, right, great, can ya drive a bulldozer? Ever driven a tractor? Can ya drive a truck? Ya can start whenever ya want, when can ya get here? Get out here, just drive to Fitzroy

Crossing, we're on the left, ask for me and we'll get you started. Rightio. See ya when ya get here.

He hung up, and all I'd managed to get out in reply was the odd mumbled *Yes*, and most of them were lies, because I'd never driven a bulldozer and had no idea what he really wanted me to do. But I ended the conversation saying yes again: I'd see him when I got there. I figured it couldn't be that hard, because I'd driven a tractor and a truck before and I'd also learned that whether I knew how to do something or not, I nearly always made a good fist of it just by trying. I was also learning to think of distance in outback terms. Alan spoke as if the mine was just a little way up the road from Broome, but Fitzroy Crossing was 700 kilometres away, and when he said *we're on the left*, he meant on the left nearly 100 kilometres *past* the crossing. The drive there alone was like crossing a European country.

Ken dropped me off there the next day. It was a lead, zinc and copper mine, and though the directions were vague you could hardly miss it. It was a giant mass of metal and machinery in the middle of the desert, and because we arrived after dark it was illuminated by massive floodlights. I felt like I'd landed on the moon to find someone was already there, building a city. Here I was again, back in the middle of nowhere, and the familiar charge of excitement shot through me. I just needed to find Alan Trotter.

Alan appeared soon enough, and as if landing on the moon wasn't enough I was surprised to find that my new boss was Willie Nelson. He was a wiry, leathery, rough, middle-aged man who looked as if he'd been carved out of the rock, topped off by long hair in a ponytail and a hat. When I introduced myself, he had no idea who I was. It took a minute before he remembered that we'd spoken the day before. Then he started running in the other direction, yelling at me to follow. He was taking me to the mess shed for something to eat, and I realised that he wasn't running at all. That was how Alan *walked*, as if something was terribly wrong somewhere and he had to get there in a hurry to fix it.

I all but broke into a jog to keep up with Alan. We sat down to eat, and he shovelled food into his mouth as quickly as he walked and talked. Seeing him do all three at once would have been frightening, because it made me nervous enough just watching him eat and speak. I confessed that I'd never actually driven a bulldozer, but told him I had been in charge of large machinery before. He seemed unfazed.

Right. I'll take ya down, give ya a quick lesson and get ya started.

It was approaching midnight by then but I soon learned time didn't matter here. The mine worked around the clock and you were as likely to start work in the middle of the night as in the morning. The dark didn't bother me; the D9 bulldozer he gestured to did. It was the size of a small house, and my job was to use it to shift earth in one of the tailings dams that collected the waste from the mine. The D9 is close to as big as a dozer gets, a 50,000-kilogram monster that comes with an enormous blade at the front, six hydraulic arms and sometimes a ripper at the back. I don't know what Alan was doing letting me anywhere near the thing, but I couldn't back out now. I was given a cursory lesson in how to operate it, and then he left me to it.

Rightio, off ya go, see how many hours you can do, we'll see ya in the morning.

And off he went again, at a furious speed. With Alan out of sight, I tried to slow everything right down, and with heart in throat started to shift great piles of dirt. I worked solidly till sunrise, unsure when to stop but in desperate need of sleep. I'd been up for 24 hours and thought I'd done well – at least I had got through the night without a major disaster. Just after dawn, Alan re-appeared.

Well, he said. *I woulda expected ya to do a fuckin' lot more than that. Anyway, knock off now and go and have brekky.*

Okay, will do, I said.

Then added, silently to myself: *Adam, what the bloody hell are you doing here?*

I SOON got the hang of the bulldozer, and the money made it worthwhile even if the drudgery of the work and the long hours didn't. Alan was paying me $20 an hour, cash in hand to be paid when I left, and he made it clear I was free to go whenever I chose. *Leave today, leave tomorra, leave in three months if you want,* he said. He seemed to be a law unto himself. He was a contractor to the mine, and I doubt they had much idea how he ran his operation. That he'd put me in charge of a D9 bulldozer after 15 minutes' instruction suggested occupational health and safety was not in the forefront of his mind.

The length of the shifts seemed excessive given the nature of the work: after a few hours driving a giant dozer back and forth under floodlights, you become a giant dozer yourself. Other workers and I were known to nod off in the cabin. We weren't driving the machine at speed and there wasn't much to crash into, but I'd been warned there were water pockets under the pit we were digging and that if I hit one, I'd sink. One night I did, and managed to clamber out of the driver's cabin just as the dozer sank below ground level into the mush. It took them three days to get it out again and Alan was so furious I feared he might beat me to a pulp, but everyone else assured me I wasn't to blame: Alan shouldn't have been putting young, inexperienced workers in charge of machines like that for such long stretches. But he was a wild man and none of that meant anything to him. Judging by the way he careered around as if he was being permanently chased by men with guns, he was in too much of a rush to stop and think about it.

I liked him, though. Alan just was what he was, a legend of the west, and though I didn't know it at the time my association with him would prove pivotal. It was the unlikeliest place for it to happen, but it was while working at the mine that I was led back to horses. Alan knew station owners in the Kimberleys, cattle farmers whose land spread across hundreds of thousands of square kilometres. He took me out several times and I was on horseback again as quickly as they could give me a saddle. Since the accident I'd ridden only sporadically but neither the passion nor the ability had suffered. I helped with mustering and watched horses being broken in, and straight away I felt a twinge: *this is what I should be doing.* I'd been on horseback almost since I could walk and it was the one constant that had survived every other upheaval.

Back at the mine, I became good mates with a young driver, also from New South Wales. Jeremy was a horseman, too. One weekend he was driving to Kununurra, 650 kilometres north-east, to compete in a rodeo. Did I want to come? Of course I did. As usual, I pretended to know more about what I was about to do than I actually did. I'd been to *watch* a rodeo, but as far as Jeremy was concerned I'd also ridden in one before. He knew the organisers of the event, and managed to get me a late entry. Fortunately I'd gilded the lily only so far, so he signed me up in the novice section, where riders without much of a clue can have a go before the main event.

The Kununurra rodeo grounds were teeming with people, and most of them seemed to have some idea what they were doing; at some point I'd have to tell Jeremy that I had none, but we weren't scheduled to ride until the Sunday so I had some time up my sleeve before confessing. I still had no plans to back out, but I figured I'd better at least get some tips on how to survive. Fear aside, I found just being there an adrenaline rush. Kununurra was abuzz, and while it was festive, the sense of celebration was tinged with an air of danger. This was rough country with rough people, and the party was fuelled by enough grog to set the place on fire. The black fellas lazed about, poor, drunk and angry; the white fellas were just drunk and angry. As we joined the throng that first night, I wasn't sure which was making me more nervous, the drunken aggression around me, or the thought of the bucking horse I'd be riding the next day.

In the morning, I told Jeremy I was not as experienced as I'd said I was – in fact, I had no experience at all. He gave me the only useful advice anyone needs to ride rodeo: hold on for dear life and hope for the best. Our names were drawn and matched with horses, and then we were put into our separate chutes with our chosen beast. I sat on the horse while someone tied a flank strap around the horse's rear, behind the rib cage. It's the tightening of that strap just as the chute opens that makes the animal buck.

I was sweating like a fast-running tap when the announcer shouted: *Sutton, out of chute number one!* The strap was tightened, the gate flew open and the horse bolted into the arena, thrashing as if it had electric shocks running through it. It seemed to last an hour. It actually lasted four seconds. At the end of it, I was on my arse on the ground, having failed to meet the eight-second minimum you need to get a score from the judges. I got an automatic zero out of 100.

All I could think was: why has it taken me so long to find *this*? Being back on a horse was thrilling enough. Discovering the greatest rush of adrenaline I'd ever experienced was a revelation. As the day ended, I went to sleep exhausted but elated, and also a little scared: I dossed in my swag under Jeremy's ute, just in case the drunk and wild rodeo revellers got completely out of control.

The next morning, we drove back to the mine, but I knew my future wasn't at Fitzroy Crossing. I was dreaming of being a cowboy.

ALAN TROTTER paid me with a bag full of cash, which stunk when I opened it. I was owed $8000, but wasn't about to count it in front of him or ask why I was being paid with smelly old notes. I could only conclude that the cash had been buried, and it didn't seem smart to ask why. I took the money and ran back to Broome, where it would give me the freedom I needed to make my next move.

I spent most of the money buying a car, a Ford ute, which Ken and I planned to use for a surfing trip to Exmouth, 1500 kilometres south. In the west, that's the kind of trip you do without giving the distance much thought. Everything is a long way from everything else. At the mine, Alan once sent me on a 1300-kilometre round trip to Kununurra to get a car part, and wanted me there and back the same day, so this week-long surfing jaunt didn't seem that much of an effort. We set off in two cars – one group of blokes in a Landcruiser, Kenny and I in my ute – and got there in a hurry. The trip back a few days later was slower – my ute, second-hand but new and precious to me, got only as far as Karratha, at about the halfway point between Exmouth and Broome, and died. It would take days to get it fixed, so I left it with a mechanic and promised I'd be back in a week to pick it up. Kenny and I crammed into the Landcruiser for the rest of the trip home.

After a couple of days, I had to leave again to go back to get my car, but I had to do it alone and money was running low. I could have caught a bus but decided to hitch, and set off out of Broome in search of a ride. I walked for hours along the highway without even a sniff of a lift, which was no great surprise, because in that time I saw only a dozen cars.

I made it on foot to the first roadhouse, where all the truckies stopped for a meal and a rest, and knew my best hope was to go up to them one by one and ask for a ride. The first one said he was going the wrong way. The second one said: *Yeah, mate. No worries. Can you drive a truck?* Of course I could. Then he showed me the truck. It stretched halfway back to Broome.

*

THE LONGEST road train on record was one-and-a-half kilometres long, and though the monster that confronted me that morning was nowhere near that big it still seemed to go on forever. I didn't seriously believe he'd want me to drive it, but half an hour after I'd climbed into the cabin he let me know he wasn't kidding.

You right to drive, mate? We'll swap seats.

He was a hefty load all on his own, adding more than his fair share to the thousands of tonnes we were already hauling, but being a fat bugger didn't stop him trying to manoeuvre his way from the driver's seat to the sleeping compartment behind the seat without bothering to stop the truck. He told me to lean over and grab the giant wheel while he pushed his massive arse up off the seat, cocked one leg up as if trying to put it behind his ear and tried to slide his way back. It was like watching Homer Simpson trying to do yoga. I was about a tenth of his size, and more terrified of him falling on me and crushing me to death than I was of crashing and dying in a ball of flames. I ducked down and inched my way across the seat, past his cocked leg and flabby belly, until I was sitting in front of the wheel. He behaved as if he did this every day of the week, and perhaps he did, but I was by then properly terrified.

You only have to touch the wheel of a rig that big to sense the size of the load behind you. I felt like I was dragging the top of Western Australia behind me. The power of the thing was frightening, and I started sweating. Never let anyone tell you that driving a machine that size requires brute strength and a dull brain. What I understood quickly was that the obese and sweaty bear beside me needed the delicate feet of a ballerina and the sensitive hands of a painter to make the rig do what he wanted it to. Everything had to be handled gingerly: pushing the accelerator pedal too quickly or too slowly could wreak havoc at the back. A small error with the steering wheel had a multiplying effect as it rippled back through the trailers. A road train, he explained, could easily turn into a dancing snake, curling from one side of the road to the other. It all hinged on what you did with your hands and your feet in the cabin.

For the first 10 minutes I had the truck jolting and jarring so fiercely he shouted at me *Eh, eh, eh! How am I gonna get any fucking sleep if you drive like that!* I slowly settled down, and the rig calmed down with me.

Wake me when we're 50 kays outta Port Hedland, he said, and before long, the sound of the truck was drowned by a storm of noise from behind me. He was sprawled across the seat, his head thrown back to one side, snoring like a chainsaw. We flew past a road sign. It said: Port Hedland, 700 km. All I could do was hold on tight and hope I didn't have to swerve to avoid an oncoming camel or cow.

The cattle were kind to me, and the camels stayed out of sight. I woke the snorer up just as he'd asked me to, and we went our separate ways in Port Hedland. He couldn't take me any further because he was taking the inland road. It was long after dark and I couldn't face trying to find another ride to Exmouth that night, so spotting a lone taxi on the street, I asked the driver if he knew somewhere cheap I could crash for the night. He drove me to a nondescript-looking building and waved me out of the car, telling me the ride was free. The place turned out to be an all-night lock-up for local drunks, a community facility where the police could deposit the pissed and the homeless for a few hours while they sobered up.

The man running the lock-up was kind and, even though I wasn't drunk and disorderly, he took pity on me and gave me a bed in what was basically a small jail cell with a metal door. I was back in prison, but after spending the day driving a giant road train with a snoring whale beside me, it seemed right that I'd end it on a ridiculous note like this. Besides, I didn't care. I was buggered. He locked me in and I slept like a baby.

The next morning, I hitched another ride south to Karratha, collected my car, and drove back to Broome, relieved to be alone behind the wheel of a vehicle that didn't have a life of its own.

ALMOST ANOTHER year had passed, and I hankered for home. I'd been out of prison for nearly three years and had done more than I could ever have dreamed when I walked free, sad and scared and fearing my only future lay behind me. I'd ridden turtles and dug holes on Lizard Island, trawled for prawns, swum with sharks and wild dolphins, gone pearling, dug a dam on an outback mine, dropped from the sky to work on Aboriginal missions and driven a road train. That was a lot of living. I'd also ridden in a rodeo, and the thrill of that memory stayed with me more than any other. I wanted to get back to my horses, and see if I could find a life in the saddle.

I told Ken I was leaving, and made plans to head back east. I had my ute and decided to drive. I put a note in a backpackers' hostel in Broome, offering a ride in return for sharing the fuel costs. Jeremy and two carloads of his mates were also planning the trip, and once I'd settled on two German women as my car companions we set off in convoy for the long drive to Perth.

We took the inland road and broke up the trip with a stop on a sheep station owned by people Jeremy knew. We spent two days there riding horses and helping with the muster, then moved on to Perth, the first major city I'd been in for two years. There we checked into the place universally known as the OBH – the Ocean Beach Hotel at Cottesloe. I left the ute in the hotel carpark, along with almost everything I owned other than a few clothes. I woke the next morning to find it stolen. More than anything, I was upset at the loss of my camera and several undeveloped rolls of film. Since my adventure started, I'd been fanatical about recording every step. In that moment, I lost months of memories.

I reported the robbery, and the next day the police called to say the car had been found – minus everything in it. I could have cried, but instead I bought a 44-litre plastic drum, filled it and the ute with petrol, and pointed the car east. There were 4000 kilometres between me and Cooranbong.

I drove across the Nullarbor alone, through South Australia, Victoria and up into New South Wales. Two days later, exhausted and unannounced, I walked through Mum and Dad's front door.

Chapter 11

I'D BEEN wandering for two years, belonging nowhere because that was how I wanted it. Home had been whatever bunk I slept in, or wherever I laid my swag. It had been a journey without obvious purpose, but the lack of purpose had been a purpose in itself, because when I'd walked free from prison two years earlier there was a different man inside fighting to get out, and he needed a lot of space. The physical freedom I'd found in all those distant places had let that bloke punch his way at least partially to the surface. He still had a long way to go.

The torment of who I would love – even whether I *could* love – still sat like a dead weight in my stomach, but I'd become expert at living with that dull ache. What had seemed like big steps forward two years earlier in Cairns – the bar encounter when I turned 21, the letter to Ian Roberts – had stopped dead; I'd moved no further since. In all the months out west, I'd added just one drunken encounter with a woman to my short list of sexual experiences. But coming home, it was relief enough to know that I no longer completely hated myself, and I'd even found much about myself to like.

Mum and Dad could see it, too – they were thrilled to see me, and happy that at least I no longer displayed the sullen misery of years before. And it must have been a relief to them that at last I had a focus of sorts. I'd lit a small fire inside with the rekindled passion for horses. I'd grasped that my future somehow lay with the animals I'd loved since I could barely walk.

Visiting the cattle stations out west, I'd watched and learned enough to have a limited grasp of what was involved in taking a raw horse and breaking it in. Looking back now, I realise that I knew almost nothing, but I had an affinity for horses and a natural inclination to stretch what little knowledge I had a long way. All I was lacking was opportunity.

I found the opportunity outside the back door when I got home from Perth. Dad had an unbroken racehorse at home, and Blade was there for the experimenting. I was blessed that he was an intelligent and fast-learning horse, because after a couple of weeks of work I'd taken him from bareback to saddle, and as far as we could tell I'd done it well, making up for what I didn't know technically with confidence and understanding, and a lot of help from Dad and Mick Alchin, a friend and neighbour. For years I'd been talking to horses about my problems, but this was a revelation: I found I could talk to a horse about its problems, and fix them. I still had no broader idea of how I might apply that talent, but finding I had it was one of the most important discoveries I'd made.

The next step came easily. It was January, and two friends of Mum's were going to the country music festival in Tamworth, so I tagged along. Taking the New England Highway out west put me squarely in big stud country, a region where vast amounts of land, money and energy are devoted to rearing and riding and racing horses. I could smell the opportunity – quite literally in Tamworth itself, which for those 10 days every year becomes a breathless mix of hay and horse shit and dirty boots and beer. With thousands of others, I pitched a tent in the showgrounds and spent eight days bouncing from bar to rodeo to concert. For the first time since the days of Pony Club as a teenager, I was immersed again with that very particular breed known as *horse people*, and this time I knew I wasn't going to walk away from them again. I returned to Cooranbong knowing I'd have to leave again soon, but this time I had a plan. I was going to find a place where I could live and breathe horses.

DARYL LEIGH, the owner of a large horse stud in Scone, was looking for an assistant who knew how to break in horses. As usual, my main challenge was deciding just how far I could exaggerate my abilities. Had I done this before? *No,* would have been the strictly honest answer. I could probably have got away with a casual response of *Sort of.* But I hadn't had all those experiences of the previous three years by being careful. Hope and confidence would again have to take the place of expertise. So when I arrived at his property for the interview, I had no written evidence that I had even ridden a horse, but assured him I could do exactly what he wanted. Pressed for detail, I described my success with Blade, and was honest enough to let him know that I hadn't followed any specific training method to break him in. I couldn't be sure I'd done it the right way.

Doesn't matter which way you did it, Daryl said. *You did it your way, and it worked.*

It was a philosophy that would stay with me. I learned soon enough that every horse is different, and that every horse relates differently to different people. Daryl Leigh gave me something else that day, too, and that was a certainty that this was exactly where I wanted to be and what I wanted to be doing. When I arrived, he was on a bucking, unbroken horse in the yard. It was dusty and hot. In that setting at that moment, he was the man I wanted to become. I spent an hour with him, and he put me on a horse to see how I rode. I'd never wanted anything so badly.

I'll get back to you, he said.

He called the next day.

When can you start?

When do you want me?

I left Cooranbong again the next morning. It was the shortest trip I made in those rambling days, across just a few hundred kilometres rather than an entire continent. But it was also the longest of journeys. My destination was as much a state of mind as a place, and for the first time I thought I might be on a road I could stay on forever.

MY NEW working day started at seven and finished at five, but if Daryl had asked me to work all night I would have. I didn't even care that my pay, the minimum I could receive under the union award, was just $270 a week, a sum that made no allowance for any sort of extravagance beyond eating and travelling. What mattered was that every single day I was outdoors surrounded by horses, and that seemed pretty close to paradise. Home was a room above the pub at the Aberdeen Hotel, a 10-minute drive from the stud, and there was only joy in waking up early every day and heading down the highway to work.

Daryl was a great horseman with vast experience, and as had happened in prison with Sam and then on the trawler with Bluey, I was blessed to be under the wing of a teacher who seemed to sense my strengths and weaknesses and who was always willing to let me have a go and learn from my mistakes. Daryl knew horses backwards; I realised watching him just how much I had to learn from him, and threw myself into it with gusto. His business was taking thoroughbreds from raw to ready for racing, as I'd done with Blade at home, but at Leigh Horse Services the scale of the operation was vast. There were dozens of horses on the property at any one time, all of different backgrounds and temperaments and abilities.

The trainer's instinct mattered as much as his technique. I had the instinct; Daryl gave me the practical knowledge, including understanding a horse's body from its teeth to its feet and how to size each animal up on sight. I learned nothing more important than this: that as with humans, first impressions count, and your ability to introduce yourself to each horse is the key to your future relationship. An unhandled horse is typically filled with fear and instinctively wants to run from you, and until you can put yourself in the horse's mind and understand how he feels about you, you won't get anywhere. Then your job is to encourage him to change his mind. Daryl taught me the importance of gaining a horse's trust and respect, before trying to help him reach his potential.

I absorbed Daryl's words like a sponge, and wrung myself out every day putting them into practice. I had 10 horses under my direct care at any one time, and was riding so much that in the early weeks I worked with bandages wrapped around my calves because the skin was worn through. Halfway through each day the bandages would be soaked with blood. Elsewhere there were bumps and bruises and grazes and cuts, because you don't ride that many unbroken horses every day without biting the dust over and over again. I was no stranger to hard work, and drawing blood in the service of a job I loved satisfied rather than horrified me. Blood and bruises were the marks of a good day's work.

I'd drive home to my little room above the pub every night exhausted but satisfied, relishing the challenges of the day to come. The work was never anything less than demanding, and could only become routine if they bred horses with computers for brains and removed their hearts. That was the thrill and the joy of it. I knew that I could and would make a go of this life. I'd found my calling, and experienced the rare privilege of realising that I was able to turn a passion into a livelihood. Whether through circumstance or lack of courage, few of us ever reach that moment. I have never been less that grateful that I was able to find my passion, embrace it and carry it forward. Back then, at the beginning, that made the paltry pay packet seem irrelevant, my digs in the pub seem a palace. Money and material things could not have replaced what I was gaining every day. When I returned to the Aberdeen Hotel at night, bruised and buggered and hungry, and Faye the publican would take pity on me and slip me a free meal from the kitchen, life could seem just about perfect.

Early on, my ute, the same car that had carried me up and down the west coast and then back across the country, packed it in at last and, with no money to fix or replace it, I opted for what seemed the most obvious solution. I grabbed the only other form of transport that was close at hand: a horse. His name was Eclipse, and for two weeks I rode him back and forth to work along the highway. It was 11 kilometres in each direction, making it hard on the horse and harder on the rider, who was already spending the better part of 10 hours a day in the saddle. Everyone thought I was nuts, but I loved the absurdity of travelling to work on horseback along a major highway, and I wouldn't be talked out of it. Daryl tried, but only succeeded once or twice when I was so exhausted from the day's work that he all but forced me to spend the night at the stud.

One night in the bar, Faye's grandson Danny, who lived on a property at Sandy Creek, was having a drink. He said he had a spare room and it was mine if I wanted it. I said goodbye to Faye and the pub and moved what few possessions I had to another new home. Danny's brother Tommy was a horseman, and so were his mates. Some of them competed in rodeo. I'd never forgotten the charge of my first, failed attempt out west and I wanted to experience it again. Since every second weekend was my own, I thought here was a way to fill the days off.

Rodeo riding is a mental battle as much as a physical one, because just to take part is a triumph of bravery, or stupidity – probably both, because they often go hand in hand. The physical challenge demands strength, and the ability to understand and respond to the rhythms of the bucking

Mum and Dad on the sand at Harbord in 1965. They met on the beach, and got to know each other on many a lazy Sydney summer afternoon.

Dad with a local while on R&R in Vietnam. This was before the true reality of the war struck – he didn't know what he was getting into.

I was born to be in the saddle. My first riding experience, aged one.

Later, I graduated to the real thing: aboard Charlie, a birthday treat.

Dad taught me to love fishing, and the harbour. I was three here, taking the wheel for a while.

I learned early that the best stories are about the ones that didn't get away. I was prouder than Dad about his big catch after this trip in 1978.

My own catches were usually smaller, but no less exciting.

Dad took us kids to Queensland on holiday after he and Mum separated, but they couldn't stay apart long.

Off to school with Sally and Leah. I was nine, and big brother always led the way.

A family portrait, 1984.

Our cottage at Lane Cove, the centre of my universe as a child.

There were always girls galore at Pony Club, but jodhpurs were never my best look.

At my Year 10 formal with Ken Rockley and my date, Linda Hughes.

Three months down, three to go: Christmas Day in jail in 1994, with my family and my best mate in prison, Sam Dixon. From left to right: Mum, Dad, Nan, me, Leah, Sally and Sam, whose face has been obscured to protect his privacy.

The family flew north for a holiday while I was working in far north Queensland in 1996 and found the post-prison Adam was a happier, healthier man.

Fixing the end of the boom of the *Krar* in the Torres Strait.

At the back of the *Krar* aged 21. I sent this photograph to Ian Roberts when I wrote to him.

On the back deck of the *Krar* the day after I got beaten up in Cairns. Note the black eye.

Into another world: on walkabout with the Pantijan people in remote Western Australia.

Competing in Campdraft on Reddy, the stockhorse who didn't let me down even when I took him out chasing brumbies.

Ride 'em, cowboy: nothing matched the thrill of a bucking horse in competition.

Just mates, not stars. From left to right: Orlando Bloom, me and Heath Ledger on the set of *Ned Kelly*. I gave them riding lessons – and eventually convinced them they could canter through flames for a dramatic shot.

Leading a pack of horses head-to-tail for a scene in *Ned Kelly*.

I was back at work on the set the day after setting my face on fire at a crew party. Orlando Bloom was the first person who came to see me after the accident and took this photo.

The cowboy becomes a bushranger: a couple of times they put me in scenes as an extra, beard and all.

The *Ned Kelly* wrap party. Heath, at the back in the striped cap, and Naomi Watts, behind him, had both become good mates.

Photograph by John Burfitt, courtesy of *Sydney Star Observer*.

The Cowboy with the Big Fella – Neil McMahon, my mate and mentor. In January 2006, I told him we were meant to do something special together, I just didn't know what it might be. By May, when this photo was taken for a newspaper story, he'd introduced a TV show about my life and we were about to start writing this book. We'd worked out what the special thing was, and started a journey few mates will ever be lucky enough to share.

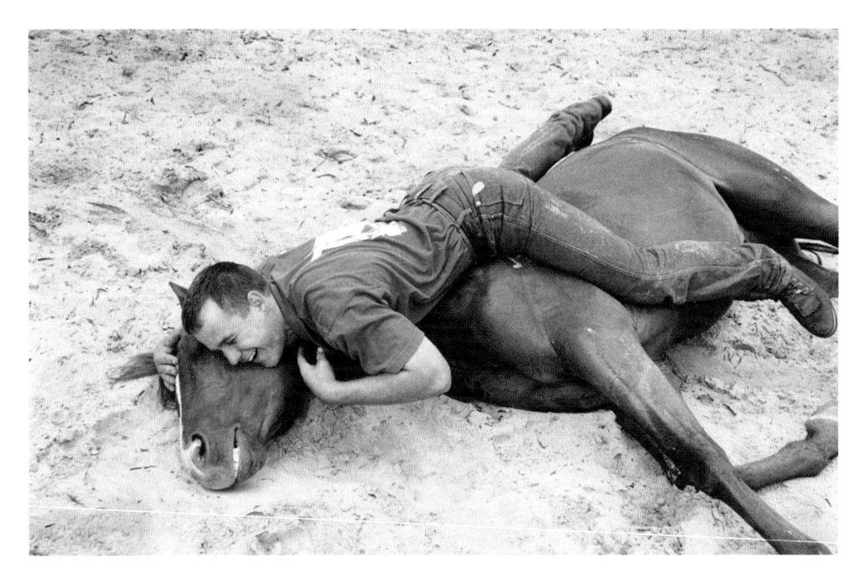

Archie and me: he is still my best mate, and for a long time was the friend I would talk to when I was still too scared to confide in people.

Practising stunts with Archie: the metal contraption behind us is the frame for the wall of fire. I taught him to ride through it when I was trying out for a Brad Pitt movie.

The next generation: me, Sally and my nephew Coby – a mischievous handful of a kid, like I was.

And the cowboy's day is done: packing up the saddles after a day's work in the yards at home.

beast. But as it all takes place in a matter of seconds it comes down to instinct more than anything else. I wanted to learn what I could, figuring I was courageous and dumb enough and that all I needed to add was technique. I got that at rodeo school.

Glen Morgan, an Australian rodeo champion, held a saddle bronc rodeo school in a nearby town. It was a three-day tutorial on how to hold on for dear life, which is essentially the skill you have to master if you want to compete. I learned that survival for the crucial eight seconds depended on becoming one with the horse, and thinking of the apparent chaos of the bucking as something more graceful: the swinging arc of a pendulum. As a horse's front feet go down and his back feet rise, your feet go forward and your body goes back, keeping in synch with the angle of the horse. It all happens in a blur, and you don't have time to ponder an if or a but or a maybe. It's rough and hard, and dangerous. I was terrible to start with, but I loved every second of it, and often a second was as long as I lasted.

There was no doubt I had the bug, though, and it didn't hurt that when I went back to work at the stud I had an endless selection of horses on hand who were more than happy to rear and buck. Unlike the rodeo horses they needed no prompting to do it. Determined to learn to stay on, I started to put myself aboard unbroken horses at work more quickly than was strictly safe for me, or good for the animal. Daryl was letting me do more with less and less supervision, and every day I'd go to work with the intention of being flung and thrown and kicked and bucked. Anyone watching me thought I was mad. I'd never argue with that, but there was a method in the madness: I was learning, and slowly I was getting to where I wanted. I was finding my seat, and could stay in the middle for longer and longer.

But there was only one way to find out how good, or bad, I really was, and that was to join the rodeo circuit. Circuit is a word that hardly does it justice. It is more like a parallel world that totally absorbs everyone within it but remains a mystery to anyone looking at it from outside. It has a culture and rituals all of its own. Most people, especially those living in cities, would scarcely be aware it exists, let alone understand its scale – a calendar of events that spans the year and the country, involving thousands of diehard competitors and fervent supporters. It's a culture apart. Danger – the charge of facing it and witnessing it – is at the heart of the spectacle. It's the world of the cowboy, the fearless man in the saddle, and the romance and sentiment of the image holds at least partly true. Women compete, too, but for the men they are often there only for decoration and recreation. They cheer, they serve the drinks, and they share the swag when the night is over. On the horse or off it, it is not a world for the faint of heart or sensitive of soul.

For a man bearing my secret curse – and that's still how I was inclined to think of my sexual confusion – I was more scared of surviving the rodeo world outside the arena than in it. Entering that self-contained universe, where everyone knew everyone and you were expected to play by the rules, there was nowhere for me to hide. It wasn't enough to prove myself a man by scoring points on a bucking horse. You could be judged more harshly if you failed in the competition that started when the riding was done and the drinking began. Rodeo men were not supposed to go to bed alone.

In every other respect I fitted in easily as one of the boys, and loved the excitement that went with rodeo night, the noises and smells and the air of anticipation that brought country showgrounds to life. Gasps and cheers and sighs and groans competed with the rasping voice of the announcer from the speakers, bulls and horses wrestled with cowboys in the chutes, music blared in the background, and booze flowed freely. There always seemed the possibility of a fight, and often there was more than one. There were men with hard bodies in boots and jeans and cowboy hats, and plenty of women who wanted them.

Nothing could have been simpler or harder for me. Two things had not changed since high school: I had no trouble attracting women in numbers, and I had no trouble recognising that I didn't want to have sex with them. At school, just being the subject of female attention was usually enough to get me by, because nobody really knew what anyone else was doing, and the typical teenage assumption is that other people are always getting more action than you are.

Back then, I looked like I was getting plenty. But that wasn't going to be enough in the rodeo world, where men travelled and lived and ate and drank and slept in close quarters, and shared their exploits not just openly but with great enthusiasm. There was little room for bluff.

I started travelling New South Wales and Queensland to compete on my spare weekends, and along the way became the bravest coward in the country. I'd put my body on the line on Saturday nights, conquering fear as I sat in the saddle waiting for the chute to spring open. Afterwards, I'd let shame get the better of me and submit to the one rule I didn't want to follow: sleeping with women. Had I been wiser then, I might have recognised the huge gulf between my physical courage and my emotional cowardice. I might have been strong enough to be myself – or at least had enough self-respect not to actively try to be someone else entirely. But it was all a mess. I surrendered to the pressure.

It takes a strong constitution to hate a part of yourself that much and carry on regardless, to ignore the strongest of natural impulses and even do the opposite to what it tells you to do. But there was no honour in it. At a time when I was in many ways experiencing the greatest thrills and deepest satisfaction of my life, I was still squaring off a corner of my heart and filling it with loathing. Women would come on to me, and I'd let them. If I could get away with nothing but some kissing and amateur groping I would, but when there seemed no way to avoid going further I'd take them to bed and go through the motions. Other times I'd take refuge again in grog, which gave me the simple excuse that I was too drunk to perform. There was more respect for a man who regularly passed out drunk than there would ever have been for a man who announced that he just didn't like girls.

No one ever knew. No one ever asked. And there was no one else like me, or that's how it felt. In that world full of men there surely must have been others. But I was too blind to see myself clearly, so was never going to recognise the same secret longing in someone else. All my energy went into hiding my secret.

One night, a bunch of the circuit boys and I went to watch a rodeo event at the Sydney Entertainment Centre, and decided to continue the party afterwards. We found ourselves at Taylor Square, the epicentre of gay Sydney, but we barely registered where we were until we started playing pool in a bar called The Oxford. A man walked past and brushed against me; one of the other rodeo boys saw it and commented on it.

Shit, we're in a gay bar.

The same man walked past once more and touched me again. I grabbed his hand, bent his fingers back until he was in pain and told him there'd be more to come if he touched me again. We left then, me the hero with my mates because I'd had a go at the poofters. It was one of the saddest and ugliest moments I'd experienced. I'd done it only to save myself in their eyes, and later that night when I was home alone I cried at what I'd done, hating myself for it. How could I loathe a part of myself so much that I would go to such lengths to keep it hidden?

I did at least grow to respect myself as a competitor. The first couple of events I didn't even make time, hitting the dirt before the eight seconds were up, and at one rodeo in Queensland I came off so hard I was out cold. I lay on the ground unconscious for four minutes, and remembered nothing from the moment I left the chute until I came to a few minutes later, being carried out of the arena. Everyone was cheering, and I thought I must have done well. The ambulance crew found no lasting damage, and within the hour I was at the bar drinking, standing tall. Walking away from a serious fall and knockout like that was a badge of honour, and didn't discourage me. Soon enough I was making time more often than not and, while I could see I'd never be a champion, I loved the thrill of it too much to want to give it up.

As the months went by, I was living and breathing horses seven days a week, and a year that had started with an uncertain return from Broome flew by. Daryl Leigh seemed delighted with my work, and sometimes amazed at how much I was getting done. I went at it hard and nearly always got the results he wanted. I eased his load and the horses I worked on were leaving his property well-started and ready to go to the track. By the end of the year, he'd upped my pay to $330, but as I headed home for a six-week break at Christmas, I had niggling doubts about what to do next. I'd helped break in nearly 100 horses, and he was charging $1300 for each one. It made perfect sense for him, but given my abilities I started to wonder whether it made sense for me. I'd proved myself, on the rodeo circuit and at the stud. I knew what I was capable of doing with horses. What was to stop me branching out on my own?

I went home to Cooranbong over the holiday break, and found that word had spread about where I'd been and what I'd been doing. People started asking me to work on their horses, and to fill in time over the weeks off I took on a few small jobs and charged for them. I didn't charge much, but the work was all my own and so was the money.

When Daryl called to confirm that he'd have me back for another year, I'd already made up my mind that I had to take a chance. I told him I would return, but not for the money he was paying me. I wanted him to double it. He said no, but I stood my ground, thanking him for a wonderful year and for everything he'd taught me, and telling him I wouldn't be coming back. The conversation didn't end well, as Daryl believed I was letting him down. I could see why, but I knew what I wanted to do. I had an idea and wanted to see if I could make it work.

A week later Daryl called again and said he'd changed his mind; I could have the higher wage. But it was too late. I thanked him again, then went and spoke to Dad. I was staying put, I told him – coming home to stay, at last. I wanted to start my own horse business, and would need all the help he could give me.

I think Dad was more excited than I was, and it was not just because he loved horses. Finally, he had his son back.

Chapter 12

IT WAS the start of 1999, five years since Adam Gosden had died. In many ways it seemed another lifetime and the crime of a different man, but for all that had changed and all I had grown, it had never left me and I knew it never really would. That was no bad thing, because it was only by keeping it close that I'd been able to face it, endure it and learn from it. It still drove me every day, whether to sadness or wandering or greater ambition. What I had not had to face for any real length of time was being back in Cooranbong, where the fear of judgements and whispers had helped keep me on the run for years. Now I'd come home for good, and those old doubts resurfaced. This time, I thought I could face them.

It was, in its way, as intimidating a time as my first night in prison, or the day I left the harbour in Cairns on Bluey's boat. This time the fears were simpler, yet harder to grasp. I felt I had to learn how to walk down the main street of town again with my head up and eyes forward, instead of cowed, avoiding eye contact, afraid of what I might see in other faces.

Just as hard, I was back permanently under Mum and Dad's roof for the first time since high school. Every other stay since then had been cut short by a deadline that marked my departure for somewhere – to prison, to Cairns, to Broome, to Scone. In many ways they barely knew me or the things I'd done, the ways I'd changed, the fights I'd fought with myself and my past. And then there was the guilt. There were not just those lost years to make up to my family, but lost opportunities and lost moments when they wanted to help and embrace me and I'd pushed them away. I wanted to make up for those mistakes, but I was never able to say I was sorry or tell them how grateful I was. Instead, I decided I would rebuild our relationship by offering them the man I was now, offer them deeds rather than words, and at last give them some reason to be proud.

As always, Mum and Dad were open-hearted. They had never judged me or turned me away, and perhaps they had been right all along: if they simply loved me, no matter what I did to them in return, I would one day come back brave enough to love them back and let them get to know me again. In my 25th year, we started out on that long road.

*

I HAD the idea in my head, but no money and no experience running a business. That didn't scare me as much as it might have, because it seemed to me that I was bringing a dream to life, indulging a passion. If I had horses and the space to keep and work them, the rest would follow. Despite having the room at home, we didn't have the facilities, other than some small and basic stables.

What do you need? Dad asked. He was desperately keen to make it happen.

And then we started building, fixing fences, constructing a large arena, a roundyard, tie-up bays for the horses, bigger stables, a room to store saddles and bridles, bits and girths. I put an ad in the *Cooranbong Gazette*, describing my services: breaking in, training, fixing problem horses. The phone started ringing; the horses started coming in. It was slow at first, which was how I wanted it, because I was working alone and everything took longer than it did at the stud. Working in Scone, Daryl was always on hand to solve a problem that I couldn't fix. At home, I had to do it all myself. If I was baffled by a stubborn horse or a problem I'd never seen before, I had to nut it out through trial and error, or hit the phones and ring a mate with a good horse brain for advice on how to fix it. Mick Alchin, who'd helped me with Blade, saved me more than once.

It was a steep learning curve in those early days, and I was determined everything had to be perfect. If a horse came in, I wanted it to leave doing exactly what its owner wanted.

I wanted them to drive away smiling. A small four-line ad in the paper was the only proper advertising I could afford, so I wanted every horse and every owner that left the property to be my real billboards, the posters that showed everyone else what I could do. The harder I worked, the more I realised I didn't know, and it was becoming obvious that even though I'd been riding horses since I was a kid, this would be a lifelong education. As had always been true, I had a hunger for knowledge if it concerned something I was passionate about, and I took every opportunity there was to learn.

The local campdraft club was a useful school, as well as a place to test and improve my own riding skills, and I joined soon after I started the business. Campdrafting is an offshoot of rodeo that has its roots in the Australian bush. Stockmen camped out for the night would square off against each other in contests of horsemanship, pitting their riding and cattle-rounding skills against each other in competitions to prove who was the better horseman and who had the better horse. Early last century those unofficial contests became a part of the travelling-tent rodeos that would tour the Australian countryside, and over time campdrafting became a proper sport in itself, with thousands of riders competing for thousands of dollars in prizemoney. For me, the opportunity was greater than that. Every campdrafting event brought together hundreds of potential clients, and potential teachers who could expand my knowledge. Lessons and clinics were run alongside the events, and I went to as many as I could, sucking in every piece of information I could, and learning from encounters with every imaginable type of horse and rider.

I absorbed so much information my head hurt, but the beauty of it was that I had a constant outlet. I'd take it home and try every new technique, apply each new discipline. I'd keep them, adapt them, throw them away if they didn't seem to work. I was slowly developing my own methods by taking something from here, something from there, something from my own experience and finding out what gave me results in the arena.

There was little time for a social life, beyond the friends I made and mixed with at campdraft and rodeo. I was still travelling and competing on the occasional weekend. That still meant drinking once the riding was done, then wrestling with my lack of interest in the women I encountered and seeing what won. I was getting better and better at the bluff – doing all I needed to do to keep up appearances, without often having to take it too far. I must have been good at it, because my mates never seemed to recognise the fraud. Or perhaps they were on to me and just let me live with my lie.

Whatever the case, I never considered giving up rodeo. I loved it too much, loved the mates I travelled and competed with and our total immersion in the world of horses. Little else penetrated my world. I didn't watch television, go to nightclubs, read books, see movies. Outside of rodeo and campdraft, I rarely went out, partly because I didn't want to and partly because I couldn't afford it. Any notion I'd had that I would rake in money on the scale of Daryl Leigh's business in Scone rapidly disappeared, but I didn't care. Those rewards would come with time and experience.

Starting out on my own, I was cheap, and believed I had to be if I was going to attract clients. I was also conscious that I was still a novice, too aware of my own limitations to put a high price on my skills. But word was spreading, and I started getting recommended for work that stretched me far beyond my experience. A racehorse trainer from Wyong heard about me and called out of the blue. He had a horse he wanted broken in, then taken all the way to the barrier on race day. I'd taken plenty of horses to the point that they were ready for trackwork – meaning a trainer could take them from my yard to the track for race preparations. What I'd never done was the next step, teaching that same horse how to actually run from barrier to finish line with a jockey on its back.

Have you done trackwork?

Again, the three possible answers lingered briefly in my brain.

No. Sort of. Yes.

Yes, I said.

He hired me. I spent three months with Barry and his horse, breaking them both in, because it sometimes seemed that Barry knew less than I did. The days were long, but the thrill of going to the track at Wyong before sunrise every morning was enough to keep me going, and if I struggled when the alarm went off, Dad was there to rouse me. Racehorses were his true passion, and if it was exciting to see his son working with horses it was doubly thrilling that I was now riding at the track every day. Not that I always did him, or me, proud.

I remember the first morning we trained for the jump-out, putting the horse and me behind the barrier as we waited for the gates to open. It's when a racehorse learns how to jump out, an ability he has to master completely if his skill at finishing is ever to do him any good. There were six horses and riders in the barriers that day. The jockey next to me looked over, and offered some advice: *Where are your goggles, mate? And your stirrups are a bit long.*

I ignored him. Then the barrier burst and my mount took off with the other horses. My feet blew out of my stirrups and as the pack pounded up the muddy track my eyes were caked in the storm of dirt and mud being sent skyward by the horses in front. Fortunately, I knew all about one thing – holding on to a horse for dear life – so I gripped on tightly and stayed with him. He went well, better than he should have done given that his rider was half-blind and shaking loose in the saddle, and we eventually got him to raceday and handed him over to a real jockey. He raced six times, and never won a thing. The prize was all mine, because I'd blundered my way to several more valuable lessons.

*

FROM BARRY, to friends who'd bought a pony for their son or daughter, people were happy to trust me with their horses. I was also ready to begin collecting a few of my own. With what little money I had, I started to buy one here and there, sometimes to keep but usually to break in and sell. It meant I didn't have to rely on people bringing me their horses to work on, and I could usually turn a small profit by buying a raw horse for next to nothing and turning it into a horse that was useful for something, even if it was just a casual weekend ride. I struck up a friendship with Sean and Kay Long, who lived nearby and who would funnel the untrained horses they bought through my business. It helped give me a regular income. None of this was making me rich, but I would soon learn how little money mattered.

I received a phone call out of the blue from a man who'd been given my name by someone. His mother had died, leaving five horses on her property, a load of horse gear and food in her stables, and he wanted all of it taken off his hands. I was left in no doubt that the alternative was the horses ending up as dog food or glue, so I drove out for a look, and liked them instantly. One horse in particular stood out, a colt.

Make me an offer, the man said. *I know nothing about horses and I just want them gone.*

I was almost broke, but I had to have them. I offered him $1000. He said that while he knew nothing about horses, he knew they had to be worth a fucking lot more than that.

I upped it to $1500, promising I'd take the lot away immediately, and he accepted. I walked away from the deal with $500 worth of feed from the shed, bits and piece of equipment and five horses that had cost me, if I averaged it out, less than $200 each. He could have made more, and I could have turned a big profit selling them on, but the dollar value meant nothing as I came to understand what I'd gained from the transaction.

I named the colt Archie, and he quickly became my best friend. And to know how important that was you have to understand that I felt like a man who had never really had one. As a wanderer, my ties had been irregular and incomplete. Friendships would stop and start, and sometimes vanish altogether when I moved on. Bonds had been broken when I withdrew into my shell after the accident. And at heart, the integrity of every friendship I'd ever made was compromised because of my secrets and lies. No matter how close I may have seemed to someone, there was a large part of me they would never know or understand.

I built a trusting bond with Archie that went beyond anything I'd known before – even more so than I'd done with Buddy, who by then had been put out to pasture on a friend's property. I'd talk and laugh and cry with him, and there never seemed to me any doubt that he understood what I was saying, recognised moments of happiness and sadness, and offered comfort and understanding. You may think that was all in my mind, but if it was, it hardly matters.

When I was lonely or sad or confused, I'd take him out for a ride and return having found some semblance of peace. I could lie down next to him in the stable and talk to him. I taught him tricks – to shake hands, rear up on command, play dead – but his greatest gift was the sense he offered that here was a creature I could tell everything to and trust completely. It still didn't seem possible that I could ever share that kind of bond with a human being, and as silly as it sounds all the love I had to give was being poured into the only outlet I had: my horse.

Looking back on those first years back home, it's interesting that, other than Archie, my most meaningful, memorable and significant friendship was with a teenager who approached me after a riding clinic on a campdraft weekend and bombarded me with questions. Warwick was only 15, but had the same intense passion for horses I'd had since childhood. I was too busy to talk to him that day, but told him to come to the house the next weekend and I'd spend some time with him.

I saw something of myself in Warwick, in his bottomless hunger for knowledge, and love for animals, and he became a regular visitor, then a constant companion. He'd spend weekends and holidays working with me at home, and then started coming to campdraft and rodeo weekends, too. He looked up to me, and seemed to think I knew it all. For me, he was a mate whose age made the friendship simple, because he didn't ask questions about my personal life, or even show any sign of wondering about it. He was as uncomplicated as Archie. I did agonise over what it said about me that my closest friends were a teenager and a horse, but the companionship of both kept me afloat and helped paper over the parts of me that were missing.

A man who'd helped me do that in another life was Sam Dixon. All our dreams of meeting up outside prison had never materialised. I'd run away; Sam had stayed in jail. And over time I'd decided that whatever our bond had been inside, it was safer for me to stay on my new path and leave prison and everything associated with it in my past. But I still thought of him often, and towards the end of my first year in business I took a short camping break with a mate, driving north from the Central Coast to the Queensland border. I'd heard Sam was out of prison and living up that way. I managed to track down his mother, and through her found Sam. He was ecstatic that I'd made contact, because there had hardly been any from either side since I'd left jail, and he told me that he had known my home address and phone number, but never used them. When I asked him why, he said he had his reasons. He didn't tell me what they were, but I guessed he'd decided it was better to leave me alone. He did confess that he was trying to make a go of life outside, but still wasn't sure he'd succeed. He didn't want his hurdles to be mine.

Sam and I spent only a few hours together, and by the time it was over I'd come to see that it was a friendship of its place and time. I still cared for him, but my life had changed beyond recognition since we were mates inside. We've never seen each other again.

Chapter 13

THE BUSINESS eventually had a name – All-Round Horsemanship – as well as a reputation, and an income that grew steadily over the first two years. It had to. In 1998 I turned over just $9000, which meant, once expenses were taken out, that I was running at a loss and only survived because I was living with Mum and Dad and running the operation from their property. In the second year, I started charging a little more and also attracted more clients. Money, confidence, experience and enthusiasm were all growing, and I kept seizing every opportunity to learn more. If I could combine learning with adventure, all the better.

An old family friend, Leigh Monnox, told me about his riding trips in the Snowy Mountains. Hearing about them, I was ready to load the horse floats then and there and head south to experience it myself. When Leigh showed me photos, it looked like a place I had been before. I hadn't, but the country was familiar to me for a reason: this was *Man From Snowy River* territory, the high country immortalised in the Banjo Paterson poem whose opening lines were more familiar to many than the first verse of the national anthem.

There was movement at the station, for the word had
passed around
That the colt from old Regret had got away
And had joined the wild bush horses – he was worth a
thousand pound,
So all the cracks had gathered to the fray.

Anyone who didn't know all the words knew the story, because in my childhood it had been turned into a movie in which Jim Craig's leap on horseback down Banjo's *terrible descent* was brought to life. I wasn't the first or last Australian horseman to imagine myself as The Man on his fabled ride across the mountains and gullies and plains of Kosciuszko. But I did turn fantasy into reality.

Leigh promised to take me along on his next trip to the Snowies, and he kept his word. Halfway through 1999, I put Reggie, another horse I'd bought, into the horse float and headed south for a three-day trip brumby-spotting in the mountains. Brumbies are the wild bush horses of Banjo's poem, descendants of the first horses brought to Australia on the First Fleet in 1788. They travel in mobs and depending on your point of view are an environmental pest, or romantic characters integral to the history of the Australian bush.

The high country was as breathtaking as I'd expected, and as perilous. It was easy to get lost, and in Australian terms it could get bitterly cold. Leigh treated this country with enough respect that he travelled with a global positioning system so he would always know where we were and how to get back to where we'd started. And he gave me a basic education in the ways of the brumby and the dangers of riding in country this wild. I learned about brumby pads – the narrow trails across mountains and through scrub that the mobs always follow – and about mud puddles – patches of wet earth that appear solid enough to ride across, but which act like quicksand once your horse sets foot in them.

After making camp and sleeping that first night, we woke before sunrise to set out for a full day's ride. Reggie was a whip-smart stockhorse with a heart that never gave in, swift and agile feet and a sharp brain that was only undone by the foolishness of the rider on his back. That first day, we approached a large patch of mud. The rule was that if you were uncertain what lay beneath, you tested it with a stick, but it looked safe enough to me. At its edge, Reggie baulked but I urged him on. He'd barely taken a step before we started to sink. I leapt off him, back to dry ground, and we managed to haul him out before he went under. I berated myself for not trusting the instincts of a horse I knew to be wiser than me about what was underfoot, but it didn't mar the most spectacular day of riding I'd ever experienced. We saw brumbies only from a distance, but returned to camp planning a bigger, faster expedition the next morning, confident the glorious weather would hold.

We woke early the next day to find our camp and everything around it covered in a light dusting of snow. It was freezing and the weather didn't improve, leaving us facing conditions beyond the abilities of some of the horses and riders in our group. We abandoned the trip that afternoon and headed for home, but I'd already made up my mind: I would go back, alone if necessary, to experience the ride I'd conquered hundreds of times already in my mind.

Later that year, I was doing well enough to take on an assistant, Brian, who had first come to me as a work experience student from a local school. He was good and keen enough that when he finished school I hired him to work with me full-time, meaning I had him and Warwick helping me out. Brian shared my adventurous spirit. I told him I'd made the trip to the Snowies once and wanted to go again; he jumped at the chance and we set about planning another assault on the high country. The week between Christmas and New Year, we packed two horses, Reggie and Reddy, into the float. Armed with whips, ropes, camping gear and food, and Banjo's poem in our minds for inspiration, we drove off for a second shot at the dream.

The trip would be as basic as could be. We didn't have the luxury of GPS, or a seasoned Snowy rider to guide us.

None of that mattered to me. We pulled up near Dead Horse Gap on the Kosciuszko Alpine Way, and set up a small camp. Our swags were our beds and, with no danger of snow at that time of year, we slept under the stars. We cooked on the fire that first night, then climbed into our swags and slept. I told Brian that tomorrow we'd be staying in the saddle until we'd ridden with the brumbies.

We set off early, and rode for hours, spotting mobs of wild horses here and there, sometimes in herds of three or four, one as large as 10, usually from a distance. We saw one mob on the horizon and plotted how we would get closer – riding down into a valley to the side, then coming around as if to circle them before coming up the other side. We guessed right, because when we popped over the rise there they were, a group of four, and when they saw us they bolted. We gave chase and came as close as I'd yet come to being in the middle of a hurtling mob, but when we got to the treeline they had us beaten and we had to end the chase. It was a long ride back to camp, tired riders aboard exhausted horses.

The next day, the gods were smiling. Riding over the tip of a rise, we were confronted by a mob that stretched 50 metres across the plain, dozens of brumbies together, and we were so close we could hear them breathe. Again, they bolted. This was the moment, and I knew it. Leaving Brian in my wake, I spurred Reggie to life and took off at a full gallop, chasing them across the flat until I drew even, then edged into the middle of the thundering herd. I was surrounded by brumbies, but they didn't kick or snarl or rear, they just kept running as fast as I had seen horses go. Reggie, as strong and determined a horse as you'd want in a chase like that, stayed with them, and while my heart was pumping I never for a second considered stopping or pulling back, even when the mob hurled forward and down, crashing headlong off the flat and into a sharp descent down an embankment.

The hooves of my horse sparked on the rock, and in that moment, as impossible and silly as it sounds, I lived a line from Banjo.

He sent the flint-stones flying, but the pony kept his feet,
He cleared the fallen timber in his stride,
And the man from Snowy River never shifted in his seat –
It was grand to see that mountain horseman ride.

Still penned in by brumbies to the front and rear and at both sides, I decided then, against all common sense, what I wanted to do next: catch one. I can't pretend I really gave it any thought, because there wasn't a second for consideration. As we headed into marshland, I went to grab my rope but it was tied poorly. I lost my grip and it fell away and was lost in the battalion of horses' feet coming up behind me. Madness took over: I pulled the left rein into my right hand and galloped alongside a small and slower member of the mob. There was nothing but the most extreme surge of adrenaline guiding me then, and I leapt off Reggie's back and aimed myself squarely for the brumby at my side, gripping him around the neck while my right hand kept hold of the single rein that kept me attached to my own mount. I had my arms around the wild horse's neck. Reggie dragged me a short way, then slowed up, and the brumby wrestled and kicked until Brian came up from behind, finally catching up to find his boss torn on the ground between two bewildered horses.

The mob left us in their dust, and as I looked at the horse I'd captured I wondered what on earth I'd done it for, and what I could possibly do next. It was, I'll confess, illegal to go brumby running in a national park, but it's been happening for decades and I can't think of what I did as cruel. For all their status as icons of bush folklore, brumbies have long been trapped and shot, dying at the hand of man, sometimes as government policy. Although they're often treated as a menace, I love them for their spirit, which I've sometimes thought echoes my own, and as a horseman they offered one of the ultimate thrills and tests of nerve and skill. I kept the horse I'd caught, named her Brumbette and took her home. I kept her wild for years, but she was gentle by nature and I eventually broke her in and passed her to a good home.

I don't often talk about the brumby run, and how I caught her – not because what I did was against the law, but because those moments riding within the wild mob seemed somehow too extraordinary to explain to anyone who wasn't there.

Chapter 14

I WAS not often surprised by the things that happened to me and the strange roads I found myself taking. The years since prison had taught me to plan as little as possible, and to always grab hold of the unexpected opportunity and unusual adventure. I'd had plenty of both and most of them had been worthwhile, or at least memorable. Then in early 2002 came the most unexpected and unusual chance of all, and even I had to stop and wonder at my luck.

It started with a conversation in the yard. Mandy Amos was a client who had brought several horses to me and was always happy with the work I'd done. This time she wanted to do me a favour. She had a friend, Evanne Chesson, who ran a major wrangling business in Victoria, supplying animals of almost every description to film companies, along with the experts to train and care for them. There was a major production starting in a few months, and Mandy knew Evanne needed staff to work with the horses. If I was interested, she'd recommend me for a wrangler's job.

The film was *Ned Kelly*, which had a budget in the tens of millions, making it one of the most expensive movies ever made in Australia, and it came with a cast that justified the investment. Heath Ledger, a young actor from Western Australia who had already made a splash in Hollywood, had signed to play the bushranger. British actor Orlando Bloom, who had just filmed part of the *Lord of the Rings* trilogy, was on board as Joseph Byrne, Ned Kelly's right-hand man. Australian stars Geoffrey Rush, Rachel Griffiths and Naomi Watts had also committed to the project. But I knew little about all that then. I didn't often go to the movies, rarely watched television and had little time for reading newspapers or magazines.

I can't remember now whether Evanne told me about the big budget and the star-studded cast when we first spoke; the names would barely have registered anyway. To me, what she was offering was an extraordinary professional opportunity and another personal adventure, and by that time I needed both. The business was three years old then and going well, but it had consumed me from the beginning. After the years of travelling and being far from home for long periods, I hadn't been away at all other than my short rodeo and campdraft trips on weekends. I was hungry for a break. And financially, it was a godsend – a regular income, minimal expenses. The film, with a substantial weekly salary for six months, was too good a chance to pass up. All Evanne had to go on was Mandy's good word followed by a single phone conversation with me, but she took a chance and hired me. This time, there was no need to exaggerate my experience. I had no doubt that I could do everything she expected of me.

Evanne gave me my starting date and, after tying up loose ends at home and closing my business for the six months I'd be away, I headed south to Victoria. Shutting up shop for that length of time was a gamble, but the sense of opportunity overrode those concerns and I comforted myself with the belief that the payoff in experience would make it worthwhile. Dad, never happier than when I was at home, busy and keeping the property alive with a stream of new horses and customers, would miss the endless activity, but he and Mum were excited for me – and by this stage of my life, I think nothing that happened to me surprised them.

By then I'd bought a gooseneck, a large trailer that is essentially a caravan combined with a horse float. It included a bed and a small kitchenette and could hold three horses in the back section, giving me – and them – a permanent mobile home. I'd been using it to travel to rodeo and campdraft events on weekends, and it gave me an added selling point with Evanne: I could sleep on site for the duration of production and look after the four-legged cast. All the horses I'd be working with were waiting for me at Evanne's property in Spring Hill, in the Macedon Ranges an hour north-west of Melbourne, and she wanted me there six weeks before production started. I drove down alone, arriving at a farm that was more like a small zoo.

Evanne's company, Australian Movie Livestock, was a one-stop shop for movie-makers in need of animals. Her film credits ranged from providing the horses for *Phar Lap* and the camels for *Mad Max 3* to the emus and kangaroos for *Holy Smoke* and the dingo that took Azaria Chamberlain in *Evil Angels*. She could answer a call for monkeys, macaws, dogs and cows, and much else besides. I'd never seen a collection like it.

For *Ned Kelly*, Evanne was contracted to provide every kind of animal the script demanded, as well as the trainers and equipment to manage them through a long, demanding shoot that would extend through the Victorian winter. I'd never been near a film set before, but that challenge was still a few weeks away. There was much pre-production work to be done first, and on that first day Evanne took me around the property and pointed to about a dozen horses in the paddocks. *That's where you start*, she said. Every one of them had to be broken in by the first day of shooting.

THAT WAS not the first or last moment I could have been intimidated during the *Ned Kelly* shoot, but I stuck with the philosophy that had served me well before: get in and have a go. It can sound *too* simple. For me, it was just simple enough. And besides, breaking in a dozen horses so quickly was far from the biggest challenge in those first few weeks; breaking in the actors who would have to ride them looked for a time as though it might be the task that really stretched me. Four of them were coming for riding lessons, Evanne told me. Only one of them, Heath Ledger, had done much serious riding before, and I had only a few weeks to get them all up to speed before filming started.

Evanne had two rules: don't fraternise with the actors away from work, and at all times during riding lessons and rehearsals, make sure the stars wear helmets. It would be too costly in time and money if any of them were to be injured.

Evanne and I quickly developed a strong relationship, and she could see I was a hard worker who was getting fast results with the horses. I respected her as a boss and as a trainer, and was ready to follow her rules. If she'd known me better, she might have guessed that would never last.

THEY ARRIVED early one morning – Heath, Orlando and two actors playing other members of the Kelly Gang, Irishman Laurence Kinlan and British actor Phil Barantini. The names meant little to me – Heath was the only one I knew much about, and that wasn't a lot. Regardless, I was not by nature impressed by stature or money or fame. It was something I'd absorbed as a teenager, when Lindy and Michael

Chamberlain's son Aidan, who lived near us in Cooranbong, became a mate. I knew of his family history, and that the Chamberlains were a family known on every street in Australia. But I never let it affect the way I treated him, and couldn't understand why so many others did, pointing and staring behind his back when he'd come on a camping trip or to a party. Later, surviving prison honed that ability: to take every man how you find him, and not be impressed or scornful based on what you imagine he might be like.

These were just four men who'd come to me for a horse-riding lesson. How hard could it be? I'd lived side by side with murderers, robbers and drug dealers in jail, dealing with movie stars seemed a doddle by comparison. Then I tried to tell them what to do, and discovered that movie stars don't always like being told what's good for them.

It all started when they refused to wear helmets. I can't remember now who led the revolt, but I stood my ground and told them there was no point arguing: if they were going to get on a horse under my instruction, they were going to put a helmet on. I was hardly an ideal advertisement for horse safety, because I rarely wore one myself, and in Heath's case I understood why he thought it was unnecessary. He'd already ridden extensively on film, in *The Patriot* with Mel Gibson and later in *A Knight's Tale*. But I wouldn't budge. They wouldn't budge. There was a walk-out, or at least a walk-off. They returned to their cars and phone calls were made. Evanne got involved, and discussions were held with the producers, who remained insistent. These were issues of safety and insurance; the helmets had to be worn.

The standoff continued for several hours, with me on the sidelines twiddling my thumbs and powerless to do anything. In the end, the bosses won. The rebellion was quashed, and the boys came back that afternoon to start again, all of them wearing the proper headgear. To my relief, the revolt was only a blip, and from then on the lessons and my pupils were a joy. They listened intently, asked smart questions and I suspect they cottoned on quickly that I was not a strict taskmaster. I never regarded riding as work and believed it should always be fun, and as far as I could I made sure it was for them. I had them careering around an obstacle course made of hay bales, racing one another and pushing themselves and their horses as far as they could. It was baffling to me that the riding lessons had been left until this late hour, and surely must have made them nervous, because they were the ones who would soon have to show off their skills on camera. But that urgency and their enthusiasm made the job easier, not harder, and I was amazed at how quickly they improved. We'd been given a detailed rundown of precisely what the script demanded of them, and tailored every lesson to those demands. I wanted to hand them over at the end knowing there was nothing the director would ask of them that they had not been taught.

Orlando possessed not a single air or grace, and in those early days and later seemed always determined to show people respect, rather than to demand it. Because of his experience, Heath was the easiest student of them all. My main job was to adjust his technique and erase all traces of American riding habits to make him a credible Australian bushranger. He struck me from the start as smart, laconic, funny, a little shy, and dedicated to getting a job done properly and quickly. As the best rider of the group, he only came to me for three lessons. We got on well, but there was no reason to expect I'd have much more to do with him beyond occasional encounters on set. Besides, my instructions were clear: don't make friends with the actors.

MICHAEL FOND was in his fifties, bearded, physically imposing, blunt but friendly, and when he arrived at Evanne's property I had no idea who he was. All Evanne had told me was that someone attached to the film wanted to inspect the horses, and it wasn't an actor needing a lesson. I showed him the horses the actors had been on, and then he asked if we could go for a ride. It was obvious that he was confident and experienced; this was a pleasure ride, and I had no problem with that – it gave me an afternoon free of responsibility. It was also an encounter that planted the seed for a deep and enduring friendship.

Michael and I made an instant connection, and what made it unusual was that it had little to do with the only thing we really had in common, which was horses. He had grown up on a farm in South Australia, but was almost

30 years older than me, had lived in Los Angeles since before I was born and moved in a completely different world. He drilled me with questions: who was I, where was I from, what was my experience? We rode for an hour-and-a-half, with barely a lull in conversation. We touched on nothing particularly personal, then or for a long while afterwards, and it was only much later that we'd discover why we both had reason to avoid delving too deeply. But it didn't matter; we shared a sense of humour that tended towards the ridiculous, and his straightforward confidence put me at ease.

I soon found out where he fitted in: he was a friend of Heath's who was working on the production. Once an actor himself, Michael had lived in LA for so long he was extraordinarily well-connected. He knew how Hollywood worked and how to get things done. When our ride ended, we swapped numbers and he returned to Melbourne, where the cast was based for the duration of the shoot. He left me with a standing invitation: when you get a day off, come to the city and visit me.

The pre-production work was hard, the days long and the pressure intense. I had every second weekend off, and the first chance I had after meeting Michael I called him to see if his invitation still stood. It did, and I jumped at it. On the Saturday morning I was on the road to Melbourne. Evanne's rules were about to be broken, but I didn't think of it that way then. I didn't think much about what I was doing at all. I'd best describe myself as clueless, and the extent to which I simply blundered into a different world is clear when I think back to that first visit.

I'd spent barely a day in a big city since we left Sydney when I was a kid, and I was a fish out of water, like Crocodile Dundee when he landed in New York. Melbourne is no New York, but it was bewildering enough for me. The traffic, the noise and the crowds threw me. I didn't understand some of the peculiar Victorian road rules, like executing a right-hand turn from the left-hand side of a major intersection – you have to see that to believe it, and it's beyond my ability to explain here. But it has something to do with trams, and I didn't know about them either: they hurtled along tracks in the middle of the road before suddenly stopping to eject passengers into oncoming traffic.

When I finally found my destination – St Kilda, by the bay on the city's edge – I didn't know why the car in front of me had stopped, or why the young woman in the mini-skirt on the side of the road was leaning in the window to talk to the driver. I didn't know why she was so angry at me for pulling up behind the car and stopping to check my street directory. Eventually the car drove off without her in it, and she came storming towards me, abusing me for scaring away her client. *He thought you were my fucking pimp,* she screamed as she bolted towards my open window.

Michael was staying in an apartment complex in Fitzroy Street. I pulled my giant Landcruiser into the parking garage next door, got through the boomgate but had to stop when the garage attendant came running out to tell me in broken English that my vehicle was too big.

Too high, you not park there, mister. Back, back.

So I reversed, smashing right into the wooden boomgate and breaking it, prompting the second burst of hysteria and abuse I'd endured in the space of 10 Melbourne minutes. I called Michael to tell him I was in strife downstairs, then set about placating the distraught garage attendant by pulling out my toolbox to perform a quick repair job on the broken boom. Michael came down, digested the scene in front of him and shook his head. I was still dressed in my standard cowboy uniform from work. To me it was normal; in St Kilda it was fancy dress. I was driving a vehicle that looked out of place anywhere other than on a farm, and was trying to calm a distressed young Asian man who was on the verge of tears because I'd broken his boomgate. Michael had the slightly worried look of a man wondering what he'd let himself in for, and from that day on I had a new name that's stuck ever since. He christened me Bushy.

The weekend was a whirlwind. That afternoon, Michael and I ran into two women on the street in St Kilda. I assumed they were somehow connected to the film, but neither name meant anything to me when Michael introduced us. They were laden with shopping bags and we offered to help carry them home. We walked with them to a house nearby, and when we got inside Michael asked if I'd mind waiting there while he went outside to attend to another job. I sat down with the two women and started chatting. They wanted to know all about me: where I was from, what I did, how I was enjoying working on the movie.

Manners dictated that I show some interest in return.

And what do you do? I asked the unassuming, petite blonde woman sitting opposite me.

I'm the leading lady, she replied, smiling.

I like to think Naomi Watts found it refreshing that I had no idea who she was.

LIFE WITH Michael Fond was like that. I never knew who I was going to meet or what might happen next. That night, we had dinner with Heath and some friends, and I was made immediately welcome. By the end of that first weekend I knew it was not the last time I'd be invited into that world. If anything, I think I was welcomed so openly because of my naïveté, rather than in spite of it. It was obvious I had no ulterior motive – I was so far from being a star-gazer that I barely knew who the stars were – and my fast-growing friendship with Michael was a stamp of approval on its own. He was well-liked and respected by everyone, and I won easy acceptance by association.

Besides, *he* was the reason I wanted to be there, not them. I loved spending time with him, and the pattern of our friendship was set that weekend. It had its foundations in our shared love of being as silly as we could whenever we could, and I learned from the first day in Melbourne just how entertaining it could be to walk a city street with Michael at my side, particularly in a place like St Kilda, where the inner-city street life provided plenty of fodder and endless amusement. He was always on the lookout for the absurd, and if he didn't see it he enjoyed creating it. Random conversations with strangers on the street or in a café were one of his favourite things, and if he could stun or surprise them with a remark or an eccentric question he loved it all the more. He was never short of an unexpected declaration, and one of his favourites was *Do you want to arm wrestle*? He had the forearms to prove that he took it seriously. He loved laying that title on unwitting strangers and then challenging them to a bout, or getting two random men to square off across a table under his guidance. Nothing ever surprised me, and together he and I could carry on like a couple of wayward schoolboys.

After that weekend I went back to work happy and relaxed, and overjoyed that however difficult or demanding the next few months proved to be, I'd be okay because I'd found a remarkable new mate.

IT WAS a hard few weeks' work, but by the time the first day of filming rolled around in May we had the horses broken in and, given the short preparation time, the actors were as good as they were going to get in the saddle. The first day of shooting took place in the You Yangs, a mountain range south-west of Melbourne, and for me it meant a crash course in the strange and demanding world of making movies. Nothing can quite prepare you for what is involved in shooting a big-budget film – the number of people, the amount of money, and the time it takes to complete what on the surface appear to be straightforward tasks. In every sense it is a world of make-believe, where the end comes at the beginning and reality is whatever the director wants it to be. Young men are turned into old ones, entire towns are built from scratch. If you need rain, you make it yourself. I remember being amazed at the scale and detail of the sets that had been built, and then discovering that almost everything was a façade. Open a door and there'd be nothing behind it; pick up a rock and you'd find it was made of fibreglass.

The first scenes we shot were from the last pages of the script, depicting the famous siege of Glenrowan when Ned Kelly is captured. The working day began at nightfall and finished after sunrise, but I was so exhilarated just to be there that I didn't notice the time. Scenes were shot, reshot, then shot again, from different angles, in different light, in close-up and from afar.

My job, along with the other animal wranglers, was to have the horses prepared, ensure the actors knew what they had to do in each scene, and be waiting just off-camera to take the horses off their hands until they were needed again.

Some of the horses were used to the activity and distractions of a film set; others needed to adjust to the lights and noise and crowds. But I was relieved to find that the horses we'd broken in handled their first night on set well, and that the actors were able to do everything the script demanded of them on horseback. It was a huge achievement for me, but one that passed unremarked and without compliment. That was a valuable lesson in itself. In an operation this vast, it seemed that the key to success lay in my work *not* being noticed; it had to be a seamless part of the complicated whole. As someone who had spent years working either alone or with only a handful of others, this was my first real experience of being that small cog in a large machine, just one of the anonymous many.

In those first weeks I worked, ate and slept on set, living in my gooseneck and looking after the horses around the clock. As wranglers, our work didn't end when the director called *That's a wrap* on the final scene of the day. The horses still had to be cleaned, fed, rugged and put away for the night. The shortest working day lasted 12 hours and many went way beyond that.

When I had time off, I was desperate for a break from the animals and from sleeping night after night in the horse trailer. There was only one place I ever wanted to go in my spare time. During pre-production I'd made another visit to Melbourne to stay with Michael, and was well acquainted with Heath, Naomi and some of the other actors by the time filming started. The trips to St Kilda continued once shooting began. I tried not to let it be widely known, mainly because I thought it better that Evanne remain unaware of what I was doing. In a sense I understood why she had her rules. She employed a team, and she wanted the team to work like one. And I didn't want to cause trouble in a world with its own peculiar hierarchy and blend of egos.

I was building strong friendships with the other wranglers, too. Martin Addy, a horseman from Queensland, became a good mate from the moment we met, as did Claire Pollock, whose friendship I treasure to this day. But I'd see Michael, Heath and Orlando on set, and it was plain my relationship with them had moved beyond the professional. Evanne eventually twigged, and while she never said anything to me directly I sensed she was not impressed. For a time she assigned me to duties away from the set, and I assumed that was the reason. I could hardly blame her. But I didn't take the cautious step of cutting my ties and stopping my weekend trips to Melbourne. I was enjoying myself too much, and even if I'd tried to back away Michael would never have stood for it. He was not a man for following rules.

But the resentment my friendship with Michael and some of the cast could have caused never surfaced. Michael was universally popular with the crew, and no one was inclined to begrudge me a friendship with him. In fact, soon enough the nickname he'd bestowed on me spread far and wide. In many ways, those months on *Ned Kelly* were like a return to my teenage years – Crazy Adam was now Mad Bushy, and I was never far from mischief or trouble.

I had three major disasters during shooting, and they happened in quick succession. One Saturday there was a party for the wrangling crew, held outdoors on a property near Evanne's place. It was the middle of the Victorian winter, and having held many similar parties at home I decided that what we lacked was a bonfire. All I needed was a place to light it, and a large pit appeared to offer the perfect spot. It was already stacked with wood, but how to ignite it? A trail of petrol from the bottom of the pit, leading out to a safe distance away, would do the trick.

The idea was to light the petrol at the start of the trail, let the flame spread along the ground, down into the pit, under the woodpile and then watch as the inferno sprung to life. It would spread warmth far and wide. What I hadn't counted on was the build-up of fumes hanging invisibly in the hole. By the time I'd laid the trail the pit had become a bomb waiting for the wick to be ignited. I lit the flame and within seconds there was an explosion that we later learned was heard by distant neighbours. Standing alone at the end of the fuel trail, I bore the brunt. The flames tore across the top half of my body, scorching my face and leaving my torso unharmed only because I was wearing three jackets to keep out the cold. The top layer of clothing melted. My head was burned, scalded through the inch of my hairline that wasn't covered by a hat.

The fireball calmed as quickly as it had erupted, but my agony was growing by the second. They rushed me inside and smothered me with cold water, which masked rather than eased the pain. Once the water stopped, I realised how much pain I was in and as the minutes went by the throbbing only got worse. I am by nature a very brave fool at times like that, and did all I could to resist being taken to hospital. But they insisted, and rather than wait for an ambulance I was pushed into a car and driven to the nearest major hospital. On the way a police car pulled us over for speeding, then took one look at my blistering face and waved us on with an admonition to slow down.

By the time we got to Kyneton hospital, my head looked like a tomato pulled from a deep fryer and I think the only thing that saved me from permanent scarring was that the flames had attacked me only for the instant of the sudden explosion. I spent the night in hospital but left the next day, sore and sorry and a scary sight.

The next day, Monday, I was back on set, determined not to miss a day. Michael Fond was among the first to spot me. I hadn't told him yet what I'd done. *Bushy!* he cried. *I didn't know they were filming scenes like that today!* At first glance Michael had assumed I was an actor fresh from the make-up room.

Word spread quickly, and by day's end the tale had been told, embellished and laughed at across the set. Orlando, ever considerate, was among the first to seek me out to see if

I was okay. My face slowly peeled away in great red slabs of burned skin, but I worked right through.

The following Saturday, exactly a week after the fire, I did my best to burnish my own legend. We had a skittish horse, and rather than leave it till the next day I decided late that afternoon to resolve the problem then and there. When he threw me forward over his head a few minutes into the ride, I wished I'd waited. The pain of the week before paled to nothing compared to the agony of a thoroughly dislocated shoulder. The joint was hanging closer to the elbow than my neck, and for the second Saturday night running I found myself being rushed to hospital with Claire, a nurse, driving. It was the same hospital I'd been to the previous week, and the same nurse was on duty. Visits on successive weekends for different disasters was bewildering even to a woman of her emergency-ward experience. The shoulder injury defeated her – it was so bad they made me go to a larger hospital in Melbourne – and me: I had to take a week off work, and I spent it all in Melbourne with Michael.

When I returned to work, Evanne sensibly showed me little sympathy and put me straight back to work in the paddocks. She put up with a lot. While staying on set in the You Yangs, I woke to find the horses had broken through a fence overnight. Thirty of them were on the loose and it took me and all the other wranglers to round them up before Evanne arrived. Then, towards the end of the shoot, I stunned the entire set at three in the morning when I bogged a truck laden with horses on the side of the highway leading back to Spring Hill. Every one of them had to be unloaded, and the reaction was universal: what's Bushy done now? It was just like being back at high school.

There was another echo of old times, too: my personal life remained a no-go area, with the crazy man still serving as my cover. There were opportunities for liaisons with female members of the crew, but I never came close to acting on any of them. I'd forced myself down that path too many times on rodeo trips and was not about to inflict the torture on myself again, especially when there was no outside pressure to do it. What never came up, and what I never looked for, were encounters with men. It was a film set, so there must have been many gay men close by, but I never knew them, or sought them out. By then, my discipline was total.

It was six years since my sole gay sexual experience as an adult, the night of my 21st in Cairns. It was a period of crushing denial that seems extraordinary to anyone else when I speak of it, and which even I find hard to fathom today. I can only explain it by saying that back then it seemed to get easier rather than harder as time went on. You don't miss what you've never had, and I had grown used to being almost completely non-sexual. My only active organ was my eyes, which could still look at a man with longing, and often did. But that was as far as it ever went. Some gay men who hear me describe it think I must be lying – I must have been doing *something*, somewhere, in secret. I wasn't.

Most of the time I was okay as long as I was busy, and *Ned Kelly* was one of the busiest periods of my life. And as I'd done many times, I tried to keep the loneliness at bay by drawing all my emotional sustenance from friendships. Sometimes I'd lose the battle and surrender my mind to the dreams and doubts, wondering if I could really live like this forever. I think I knew the answer well enough, but still wasn't ready to accept it.

The strange thing looking back is that I'd never mixed with such a worldly crowd, or had a group of friends more willing to accept that part of me without judgement. These were not country people who found homosexuality foreign and frightening. I guess the point is that I very much still was. I've learned since then that the true torture of the closet is that you are at heart a prisoner of yourself – of how you see yourself, and how you *imagine* others will see you. Homophobia plays a large role, and to that extent it keeps you locked away. The problem is that you eventually see hatred even where it doesn't exist, and become a victim of something you are only guessing is waiting to harm you.

These were truths still a long way from becoming clear. I was far from wise, and I was certainly lonely underneath it all, but I can't say I was unhappy. For the duration of the shoot, life felt good nearly all of the time, even with the limitations my heart and mind were placing on it.

As the film came to an end, I could look at my life and

imagine it as a party, with everyone gathered to celebrate my success. If I excused my secret from the room, asked it to stand outside, I could look around at the gathering that remained and be grateful that I had come so far and built such remarkable friendships. Over there, Heath and Naomi – people from different worlds who'd accepted me easily and become my friends. Michael Fond – I knew then that I'd know him as long as life kept us both here. Claire – she became like another sister, and never questioned or doubted me for a second. I could bring others to the room, too, and I wished they could see the distance I'd travelled: Ken from Broome, who had never let me down; Leigh Maule, a friend I knew would never set limits; and my family, whose loyalty had withstood the hardest of tests. Conjuring that party in my mind late in the winter of 2002, it was easy to see myself as the happiest man there. Then I'd invite the secret back inside, and realise that the only person in the room who still hadn't worked out how to like me, was me.

Chapter 15

THERE HAD to be a reckoning sometime. I arrived back in Cooranbong satisfied with everything I'd achieved, but unprepared for the idea that at some point the crash would come. The career achievements of the previous six months had transformed that part of my life, and I was ready to grasp every opportunity it offered, to walk through every door it opened. The upheaval of the months to come would turn out to be nearly all personal, and some of what was thrown my way would be terrifying – opportunities I would hesitate to seize, doorways I would be scared to enter.

It didn't start out that way. It was a period that began in a professional whirlwind. Everything happened in a hurry. Soon after I got home I had a call from Sue Baldwin, a horse master from Queensland. It was a hint of another movie job. Brad Pitt was due to start shooting a science-fiction film, *The Fountain*, at the Warner Bros studios on the Gold Coast in a matter of months, and the producers needed horses trained to perform some difficult tricks and stunts. It was a feeler more than a job offer; she was talking to several different trainers, and wanted me to send in a videotape of my work with horses.

I set to work with Archie immediately. He was the one horse I had at home with the temperament to learn the tricks quickly, and who had the trust in me to understand I would not let him come to any harm. That was crucial, because among the stunts I had to teach him was to run through fire without flinching. I'd done it with several horses on *Ned Kelly*, and had even given Heath and Orlando an on-set pep talk to convince them to forgo stuntmen and run the flames on horseback, too.

You can do it, I told them. *I'll be waiting for you off camera as you come through.*

They trusted me enough that after I told them they had the skill to carry it off, they believed they could do it, and they got through it unscathed. They were proud of themselves – and I was proud of them, and of myself. That was what the film had given me: experience and knowledge to match my bravado.

I spent weeks with Archie, using a combination of my own ideas and some I'd picked up from books and training videos. Calm and clever, he took to the task with relish and I eventually had him on film romping through a wall of flame, falling over and playing dead, rearing on command and collapsing as if he had just been shot.

I finished the audition tape and sent it in, but as quickly as it had come up, it all came to nothing. Brad Pitt pulled out of the project at the last minute, and the film was put on hold indefinitely. I didn't regard it as a waste of time, though – it was work that took my relationship with Archie to a different level of trust and understanding, and I was thrilled just to have been considered for a job. It was immediate proof that *Ned Kelly* would stand me in good stead.

The film experience had only deepened my drive to broaden my experience and ability with horses. I already knew a lot, but that only made me realise how much more I had to learn and how much better I could become. In September, I wrote a letter with exactly that in mind. John Stanton was a legend in Australian horse circles, a bushman born in Tamworth who had spent most of his seven decades in the saddle. He was a champion competitor in rodeo and campdraft, and a renowned horse breeder and breaker with a property on the far north coast of New South Wales. He was also my idol. I'd met John several times at campdraft events, and he was everything I aspired to be – a master of the animals he loved.

In my letter I laid it on thick, telling John what I'd already done but explaining that there was so much more I wanted to do. *I want to keep learning,* I wrote; *to absorb knowledge from everywhere and everyone. Would you consider letting me work with you, even if just for a short time?* I sent it, not sure I would get a reply. I guessed he often received letters like that, from keen young horsemen like me wanting to learn at the master's side.

And then John called. We talked briefly, and he said *Yes*. He would take me on for a few weeks. It was more than I really expected, and all that I wanted – I could learn more from him in a month than I'd learn in a year anywhere else.

I loaded up the gooseneck once more, and drove north, thinking that the trip was going to be all about horses. How wrong I was.

THE WORK with John Stanton was everything I hoped it would be. He had his own methods of breaking and training horses, honed over decades, and there seemed to be nothing he couldn't do. I drank it all in, throwing out some of my own habits and replacing them with the techniques I absorbed from him. The days were long, often starting at sunrise and ending well after sundown, but I loved it. This was more thrilling to me than spending time with movie stars; in my mind, John Stanton was more of a celebrity and more intimidating than anyone Hollywood could throw at me. Even casual conversation with him could be a classroom; he had been around for so long and seen so much, his memories were a textbook for a pupil like me. I hardly saw anyone but him for days on end; we had 13 horses to start, and I'd learn under his wise eye. He taught me wrongs from rights, and showed me ways and whys.

One afternoon I was at the local showgrounds, where many locals kept their horses, when I spotted across a fence a good-looking young bloke in riding gear. There was enough of a spark in that first glance to make me look again. He looked back, and I walked over and struck up a conversation. We talked, as horse people always do, only about horses. Then he took me by surprise.

Do you wanna go for a beer sometime?

I said yes. His name was Jeff and he was 24. I was 28, and at last I'd stumbled into the moment that would shake everything loose inside.

We went for that beer, me nervous partly because I knew I liked him, and partly because John Stanton was a teetotaller who never went to the pub. I feared he would frown on an employee who did, but I wasn't about to stay away. It was hardly what you'd call a date. Other than my instant attraction to him, there wasn't the slightest indication that Jeff was gay, and when Thursday night rolled around and I arrived at the pub he had brought two mates with him. That was as much a relief as a disappointment, because it removed any suggestion this was anything other than some blokes meeting for a beer. We talked about nothing in particular, and when the night was over it seemed an encounter of no consequence at all.

I saw Jeff twice more before I finished my stint at the Stanton property – another meeting at the pub, and one night I went to his home. He still lived with his parents, and

I met his mother. We were to all appearances just mates, and he wasn't the first mate I'd had that I had a secret crush on. But I sensed that there *was* something else. And this time I acted on it.

Just before I left for Cooranbong, I made plans to see Jeff again. I told him I'd be back up at John Stanton's place at the end of December to collect some gear and that maybe we could go out. In fact, I had nothing to collect from John, but I needed an excuse because I was a long way from being brave enough to let Jeff think I was coming all that way just to see him.

It was only a few weeks away, and I drove home with much more than the Stanton method of horse-breaking running through my mind. But I had six weeks to wait until I'd see him again, and there was another major work challenge to be completed before then: more brumbies.

I'd long done occasional work for the local RSPCA, accompanying their inspectors to properties in the area to check on horses they believed were being maltreated. They'd take me along to help assess them, and to capture them if they needed to be removed from a bad home. It was rewarding and sometimes confronting, because the owners often maintained they'd done nothing wrong and could get aggressive when we tried to take their animals away.

This time the association contacted me with a challenge on a much larger scale. There was a mob of brumbies trapped at New Place Creek near Bucketty without food because of a bushfire. Many were dead or dying. The Department of Agriculture wanted those that were still alive captured and brought in, without the controversy that had erupted after an operation a year earlier when scores of wild horses had been shot from the air. That slaughter had been captured on film, and public outrage boiled when it was shown on television. This time, the RSPCA had been put in charge of making sure the animals were captured humanely and brought back alive. Could I do it? It was not going to be simple or cheap, but I couldn't say no.

I hired a team of four local horsemen who I knew I could trust, and in late November we headed into the park weighed down with every piece of equipment I thought we might need to round up the horses, including portable fencing and long rolls of plastic sheeting to create makeshift chutes to funnel them through from the valley that trapped them into our makeshift horse yard. When we got to the site, it was immediately obvious how dire things were – 30 horse carcasses dotted the landscape, and the brumbies that were still alive were emaciated. But that made them no tamer or easier to subdue. I gave us a realistic chance of bringing in a dozen of them.

The horses were in a relatively confined space, but they were still spread across a large area and capturing them was going to take patience and time.

To tempt them closer, we dumped bales of hay and waited for them to get comfortable. It took incredible patience, and tested me on other levels, too. I had three young men working for me out in the wild for days on end; I had to worry about their welfare as much as that of the horses, but I also knew that it was only my reputation that was at stake. I was determined not to fail, and every idea and instinct I had had paid off. Three of us rode the mob from outside; the other two waited at our camp to corral them once we got them close enough. Slowly we won the battle. We rounded them up in ones and twos, penning them in the long chute we'd erected and driving them into the yard. I had us home in eight days, 11 brumbies on board and still alive. It was one of my most satisfying achievements, and the department was as pleased with the result as I was.

DECEMBER COULDN'T go by quickly enough.

I drove up north the week after Christmas, finding it hard to believe I was doing it. I desperately wanted my instinct to be right – to find there was something more there with Jeff – but at the same time I was a bundle of nerves. I was staying at his house with his family, which in a way calmed me down once I'd arrived. It was at least a familiar, comfortable environment – a family home, me there as just his mate and a guest for the night, sleeping in the spare room. Jeff seemed pleased I'd made the trip, but there was nothing in his manner to suggest he was nervous. Part of me longed for a sign that he was, while also hoping I was not showing anything of the sort.

We headed out for the night. There was nothing unusual about it, until the bar closed. The two of us walked home, inebriated and happy, and halfway there we stopped and sat down under a tree. They were only five words, but they were the hardest I'd ever spoken.

I want to kiss you.

A kinder God would have sent that tree toppling over to crush me before I managed to get them out, or presented a hole in the ground to swallow me once I'd uttered them. Instead I had to live with the embarrassment. Jeff was horrified. He seemed stunned, offended and probably furious. I couldn't be sure, because I suddenly felt ill and was too mortified to look at him. I remember him swearing, then standing up. *I'm not like that,* he told me. It had taken me years to get to that moment, and when it arrived I'd managed to get it all wrong. We kept walking then, in silence, and when we got to his parents' house he told me gruffly that I could sleep downstairs.

I was too upset and embarrassed to go inside the house and too drunk to drive, so I stayed in the garden, eventually lying down on the trampoline with my head spinning, wanting to be anywhere else but there. I waited a few hours to sober up, then before dawn got in my car and drove to the beach. It was deserted, and I sat down on the sand and cried. All the self-hatred I'd kept at bay for years returned and washed over me so intensely it became a physical sensation. The confidence I'd possessed for just a few seconds had been shattered just as swiftly. There was nowhere to go but home, so I drove straight back to Cooranbong, humiliated and feeling further than ever from the breakthrough I craved.

I was unprepared for the anger that had been set loose. It was the same fury that had gripped me when I was a teenager and I was a nightmare to live with. It all came back, this time mixed with a frustration that I couldn't suppress. The internal intensity of the encounters with Jeff confirmed in a rush what had been dawning slowly: this was never going to change.

The idea of telling my parents was not just terrifying. It seemed an impossibility. And besides, what would I be telling them? That I was gay? I still had only the barest understanding of what that might mean. I'd had just one real sexual experience with a man, seven years earlier. I had never met a gay couple. I'd never seen a gay movie, or looked at a gay magazine. I couldn't imagine a gay man living in the world I inhabited. A gay cowboy? It seemed ridiculous. *I* seemed ridiculous. How could I be this, and also that? If I was that, how could I be *me*? These were the agonies that started consuming me, the questions I'd long ago learned to banish once they started wandering through my mind. I never asked them out loud, but something had to escape.

What seeped out was fury. It scared everyone around me, and the depth of it scared me, too. I was short-tempered and barely keeping a lid on a bubble of physical aggression that seemed about to burst. At home, it was as if I'd wound the clock back 10 years, to a time when all I did was push people away. I didn't fight with Mum and Dad, but I didn't need to for them to know something was wrong. They'd seen it before: the sour moods, the one-word answers, the snappy and curt comebacks, the downcast eyes. I'd even get angry with the horses, cursing them and kicking my boots in frustration in the dust. That was a sure sign something was wrong, but once again I was not going to let anyone in. The question was how long I could last before letting myself out.

As a man who'd spent nearly all his life outdoors, I was the unlikeliest of people to find salvation in technology. But it was the computer Mum and Dad bought for the house that gave me my release. I'd barely used one before, but I created an email account and then started clicking and exploring. I found a website that advertised itself as bringing single people together. And not just *straight* single people. The questionnaire asked me who I was and what I was looking for, so I took the leap and told them. *Male. Seeking: Male.* This was a moment of great significance to me. It was the most definitive statement of intent I'd made. I was actually *doing* something; I was exploring. It was as simple as a handful of keystrokes.

I created a profile for myself on the website, laying out the bare bones of who I was. At first the thrill came not from the possibility of contacting other people, or meeting them. That idea still terrified me. It was exciting enough just to read the things other people said about themselves, the world they described, and to register that there were so many people out there *exactly like me*. I found another world, populated by hundreds of people I had hardly dared believe existed. As far as I could tell, none of them thought there was anything to be ashamed of. They had nothing to explain. Being gay was a given.

Even though the website was a virtual world, it was still a relief to discover that there was somewhere for me to go. The website let you exchange messages with other members via email, and I made contact with a couple of people that way. I was even brave enough to speak to one on the phone. But that was as far as it went; just making the phone call took more courage than catching a wild horse.

It was exhilarating and confusing all at once. I had opportunity and choice, both of which presented their own dilemmas. For a long time the decision was crippling but simple: do nothing. Now the decision was: do something. But what?

Before long, I'd signed on to another website, this one exclusively for gay people. The Gaydar community was global, and communication was instant: I could have live online conversations with anyone who happened to be logged on at the same time, and those encounters – protected by distance and the anonymity of the computer screen – were liberating. I could reveal as much or as little about myself as I wanted to. I could ask questions, and I had many. I could express thoughts and feelings that had never passed my lips. For me, the internet and its anonymous connections were not for the sleazy and desperate, as many people imagine. Alone in the country and only starting to confront the truth about myself, this was a lifeline that might have saved me long ago had it existed when I was a bewildered teenager with no one to turn to.

I learned things every day. Most importantly I learned that there were many men like me in the Australian bush, and they were using the internet in exactly the same way. Without leaving home, they could escape. For many, it offered something precious: someone to talk to after years of silence. I started making friends. Could I be friends with someone I had never physically met? Yes, I could. I was able to be more honest about myself with them than with anyone I'd ever met in person.

Some online encounters sparked interest beyond friendship. In early February, I took the plunge and arranged to meet someone I'd spoken to many times online. Jason was the same age as me, lived in Sydney, and, judging from the photographs I'd seen on his internet profile, he was handsome. I arranged to meet him on a Sunday at Manly Beach, and to my amazement I went through with it. I was again a bundle of nerves, but we spent the afternoon together, just walking and talking.

I liked Jason; he was confident, funny, easy to be with, comfortable with who he was. How I longed to be like that. It never went further than a kiss goodbye that night, but that was enough to turn me inside out. *Can I really do this?* It was suddenly more real than it had ever been – there was a *real person* involved, a person I'd touched. There were voices pulling me back. I'd taken one step. Another would move me beyond the point of no return. Was I ready for it? My frustration should have been easing, but instead it was building. I had effectively started living two lives, and I was full of uncertainty about both. Neither life seemed able to make me completely happy; and I still couldn't fathom how they might be reconciled into one content existence. I braced myself for another brawl in my head. It was an endless wrestle with myself.

The watershed moment came the following week. Since coming home from *Ned Kelly* I'd been spending a lot of my spare time with Leigh Maule. She had always been there in my hardest days – before prison, during it, and beyond, and now she would be there again at the most important moment of all. Leigh, like Mum, was a hairdresser and they had formed a close bond over the years of our friendship. They would talk often, and I later learned that Mum had told Leigh how worried she was about me. She couldn't understand why all the difficult traits of old – the anger and aggression, the withdrawal into myself – were coming back. Mum once even asked Leigh if she thought I might be gay;

Leigh gave her the same answer I'd offered when Mum put the question to me the previous year: a categorical no.

The week after my meeting with Jason, Leigh came around one afternoon to take me to a movie. I was in the yard finishing work with a horse; she was in the kitchen talking to Mum. I'd been putting myself through days of torment yet again, swinging from high to low and back again, hating myself and riddled with fear that someone would find out, yet knowing it was what I wanted and unable to pull back. The frustration was intense, and in the yard that day I finally snapped. A horse didn't do what I wanted it to and I screamed at it, then lashed out physically. I punched a wall, kicked and yelled, smashed anything I could lay my hands on.

Mum and Leigh were watching me from inside and were distraught. *I can't watch,* Mum said, and turned away in tears. Looking back, their tears tell me only one thing: that they had been building for a while, just as mine had. They were not surprised by what they saw.

Leigh ran outside to me, and I screamed at her: *Don't come down here, or you'll be next.* But she stood her ground, and ordered me to stop. *Adam, get in the car. I'm getting you away from here now.*

She stopped me in my tracks.

We drove off and I started crying uncontrollably, while Leigh kept pressing me to tell her what was wrong. I told her I'd met someone. She said that was wonderful; in 10 years, she'd never known me to have a relationship. Then I told her who it was. I'd met a man.

I think I'm gay.

The release I felt on saying those words was a surprise even to me – the load was lifted. I'd done it, and saying it out loud suddenly made it seem all right. The sky had not fallen.

Leigh told me how happy she was, and hugged me. I couldn't believe it had happened, that I'd let the truth in to the world that I'd walled off with lies for so many years. All I was getting in return was love and happiness, not the rejection and judgement I'd feared. The anger drained away, replaced by relief and excitement and gratitude.

Leigh still remembers the words I used to describe it.

I feel so much taller now.

Chapter 16

THE FLOODGATES had opened, and it's hard to put into words how free I felt. Many gay people describe the same experience: of suddenly realising just how weighed down they had been, once that burden was lifted. Over the years I had grown accustomed to its weight, and was astonished at the lightness of my step once it was gone. I had a long way to go, of course – Mum and Dad still didn't know – but I now knew where I was going, and that I wanted to get there. I could feel the anger melting away inside.

A few weeks later, in March, Michael, Heath and Naomi returned to Australia for the *Ned Kelly* premieres in Melbourne and Sydney, and included me in their plans: I'd stay in their hotels and go to the premieres as a member of their party. I was thrilled, but Michael had long included me in everything and would have frowned at any show of gushing gratitude. We were mates, involved in each other's lives; this was his life, and there was nothing more to it than that. The conversation I did need to have with him was a different one altogether: telling him all that had happened to me and telling him the truth about who his mate was.

I flew to Melbourne in mid-March and Michael collected me from the airport. We talked casually as we drove to the city – catching up, chatting about the night ahead. Then he glanced over, and beat me to it.

Bushy, there's something I've got to tell you. I'm bisexual.

I told him my own secret in return. In all the time we'd spent together, I'd never asked and nor had he, and neither of us had made assumptions. Now that the truth was out, we just laughed at how silly we'd been, and left it at that. Nothing more needed to be said, because we both understood the strength of our friendship, and that it was now much stronger for knowing this.

I was quietly rapt. For all the contacts I'd made online, here was something of a different order: my closest mate was just like me. It was a simple thing, but I'd been a long time finding it.

For a while in those weeks, it all seemed like somebody else's life. The premieres were a whirl of excitement. I was on the VIP list, which was amusing because I was well aware how unimportant I was to the film in the larger scheme of things. But it was a buzz. The world premiere was held at the Regent Theatre, and it was about as Hollywood a moment as you'd ever find in Melbourne: stars, cameras, lights, gawking fans. The screening was followed by a party that went all night. But my lasting memory of the evening is not the glitz and the glamour. His name was Jeremy and we met online.

Jeremy lived in Melbourne, so when I knew I was coming down I asked him if he'd like to come to a party with me. I didn't tell him exactly what sort of party it was – just that we were going to a movie. I wanted to surprise him, but also didn't want to come across as trying to impress. He'd never been on a first date like it. I'd never been on a first date at all, and this was one to remember.

Jeremy was gobsmacked from start to finish, and I can't pretend I didn't enjoy being the man who did the gobsmacking. Nothing much ever came of that meeting, but I'll never forget it: turning up to a party with a bloke on my arm. Unsurprisingly, the film crowd was unfazed by my date being a man. It passed unremarked and unquestioned. It was only weeks since I'd made those tentative steps from the closet. Now everything was happening so quickly, and it was as if I'd broken into a sprint and was running away from the open door as fast as my legs would take me.

After the Sydney premiere, I went back to work at home and tried not to let my new life distract me from work. It wasn't easy. As any newly out gay man will tell you, the feeling of being a kid set loose in a candy store can be overwhelming: endless opportunity after years of denial. Although things didn't develop much further with Jason, the man who met me at Manly Beach, we stayed in touch and I was content to just let my world expand. I was online every day, chatting to new people and building on those friendships I'd already made.

The website divided its members into geographical areas, so I was able to talk to dozens of men in the country, men who lived similar lives to me – lives on the land. I found cowboys, cattlemen, sheep farmers, crop growers. I struck up a friendship with Craig Swain, a born-and-bred farmer from Nundle near Tamworth, and drove out along the New England Highway to meet him. I found a man who had suffered many of the same torments as me, and who had also just found the courage to confront them. His family and community embraced him without hesitation, and while that was a bridge I still had to cross, I learned from Craig that it could be done.

There were times I'd pinch myself at the thought that these people had been there all along, and that all of us had imagined we were alone. It was the emotional release that mattered most, not the sexual one. I did have sex occasionally, and it was wonderful to experience the excitement of physical contact with another person, openly and without guilt. After years of believing I'd never be able to properly satisfy that part of me, the relief was intense. It felt natural and normal. But what struck me was how every friendship I made, every sexual encounter I had, confronted me with everything my heart had missed, rather than my body. I learned that accepting being gay was not all about sex.

I could be celibate and still be gay; I had been for years. Now I had to learn to accept who I was and respect myself, and then to expect acceptance and respect in return. I was coming to understand that simple truth. All my walls were crumbling.

In some ways, the friendship that counted most in that period was with an old friend I didn't know was gay. Dan Lowden lived nearby in Wyee, and we'd known each other since Pony Club days as teenagers. In early 2003 I did some horse work for a friend of his, and we re-established a friendship that became pivotal.

One night he said to me: *There's something you probably haven't heard, mate. I've come out. I'm gay.*

That's cool, mate, I told him. Then added the surprise: *I think I am, too.*

Dan thought I was having him on.

I reckon you're just saying that to make me feel better.

It was the first but not the last time I'd tell someone and be disbelieved, and I had to chuckle at the silliness of it: I'd kept the secret my whole life, only to have someone think I was making it up when I finally summoned the gumption to tell them. I didn't know whether to be flattered or offended. I assured Dan I was telling the truth. He said that if I was, I'd come with him to a gay bar at The Entrance, a small seaside town halfway down the freeway towards Sydney. I took up the challenge. For everything that had happened in the previous few months, this was something I hadn't done, but if I was going to take the plunge into the world of gay nightlife this seemed as easy an opportunity as I would find.

The club at The Entrance had a gay night once a month, catering to the country crowd that didn't want to trek all the way to Sydney for a night out. Dan, still unsure whether to believe me, picked me up on the Saturday night and we drove down together. I was nervous, aware that I might run into people I knew and also realising I would be meeting new people face to face. There would be no computer screen to protect me.

We hadn't been at the club long before I met two men. The older one extended his hand, and I shook it. It was a firm handshake, with a rough, hard hand.

What do you do, mate? I asked him, knowing it had to involve some kind of physical labour.

Scotty had a brick-laying business. His boyfriend, Alex, was a mechanic. They'd been together for years, and were another lesson in my swift education that things are often not what you might expect them to be. On my first night in a gay bar, I was hanging out with a bunch of ordinary knockabout blokes.

BY JULY, I'd gone from being a man without a gay mate in the world to one who had established firm friendships. I knew a gay farmer. I knew a gay couple. Soon I'd discover that Rob Caska, my vet, was gay, too, and I became close friends with him and his partner, Sean. But it was Scotty and Alex who first took me under their wing.

I think Scotty and Alex both understood quickly that I was a handful, and needed gentle guidance. I was naïve, but also like a bull at a gate, charging forward without stopping for long to consider the consequences. For all I had changed, I was still never far from trouble. On our second night out at The Entrance, Scotty had to pull me aside and tell me to calm down; I was knocking people flying on the dance floor, and in a moment of over-exuberance had picked up Shelly Legs Diamond, a famous Sydney drag queen, and held her above my head until she all but screamed the place down.

There was another major breakthrough at that club: one night I ran into an old mate, Ben Bryant, who I knew through Pony Club years before. Benny was straight, but he ignored labels like that and being in a gay bar didn't faze him at all. Seeing me there did. When I told him the truth, he didn't blink. It was a brief moment, but a major lesson. By telling him, I hadn't lost a mate – I'd found a better one.

The next step was obvious, and Scotty and Alex made it happen: what about a night out in Sydney? That meant Oxford Street, the gay golden mile in Darlinghurst. I hadn't been there since that awful episode in a gay bar a couple of years before when I was out with the rodeo crowd. Two years on, I knew I'd moved way beyond moments of madness like that. I was ready for Sydney now, or thought I was.

I think Scotty and Alex were more worried about whether Sydney was ready for me.

Arq nightclub at that time was at the heart of Sydney's gay nightlife, the venue the community converged on late at night on weekends to party through till dawn. It was often referred to as Sydney's superclub, a place to rival the biggest and best venues in Europe and the US. I'd never seen anything like it: behind the humble and nondescript entrance in Flinders Street was a three-level palace built to feel like a corkscrew: a circular gallery at the top winding down to the main arena, and then curling down another level to a lounge area with a smaller dance floor and pool tables.

It was like stepping into another world. I couldn't believe the number of people flooding the place late on a Saturday night, or the energy that surged through as the crowd grew and the music soared. I was an innocent, though not too naïve to know that the energy was fuelled by recreational drugs. The energy was positive and uplifting, with none of the aggression you'd find in a bar where alcohol was altering the mood. It was hedonistic and narcissistic, and it was also surprisingly friendly. Everyone seemed to know everyone else, but it didn't matter if you were a stranger: people talked to you anyway. Shirts came off, and the party carried on; it was eye-popping, sensual, silly, and irresistible.

I kept my shirt on, and stuck to beer, but was exhilarated by it all anyway. As many had done before me, I found moments of absolute freedom on the dance floor, in a place that was meant for me and people like me, where I didn't have to worry what anyone thought of me or what anyone might say. That was true even though I couldn't see myself in the people around me; there was no question I was from somewhere else in my check shirt, ordinary workaday jeans and scuffed cowboy boots, nursing a schooner of Tooheys New. I was surrounded by men wearing labels – even if they wore a humble singlet it was likely to be worth more than my jeans – drinking expensive bottled water or trendy beers. I must have looked a sight, but whatever my insecurities they didn't extend to worrying about things like that. They didn't matter, and I gave Crazy Adam free rein. He'd protected me all these years, helped me survive in all the other worlds I'd rolled through. In this new world, he could stop working so hard. I didn't need him to protect me any more; instead he could just be crazy for its own sake. My two halves were becoming a whole.

I must have met dozens of people that night. They'd stare at me from a distance sometimes, wondering who the mad bastard was who didn't dance like everyone else, who jumped and hopped and spun like a washing machine on spin cycle.

But I wasn't there just for that, liberating as it was. As much as I was trying to find myself, I also knew that underneath I was searching for something else – someone else. I was 28, and still alone. I'd always been alone. I'd never held someone's hand, or bought a present for someone I cared about romantically. I'd never woken up with someone next to me. I'd never taken someone home to meet Mum and Dad. I'd never said *I love you*. No one had ever said it to me.

That was the truth at the heart of me. I wanted to love someone, and be loved back.

Chapter 17

MY PROBLEM was that I wanted it all in such a hurry. I would latch on to people with a kind of obsession, then lose interest just as quickly when someone else set my heart racing. And the organ that was racing *was* my heart. I wasn't interested in one-night stands. Sexual fulfilment interested me less than finding a balm for the emotional wound: all that loneliness, which loomed larger than ever now that I'd let myself contemplate how much it was really hurting.

On that first weekend in Sydney, I met Grant, a policeman and a decent bloke whose masculinity seemed to be exactly what I was looking for in a partner. I saw him several times and he even visited me at home – I introduced him to Mum and Dad as a mate from Sydney, nothing more – and for a while I imagined he might be the one. But there were other complications: around the same time, I struck up another relationship of sorts with a bloke who lived near

Cooranbong. We'd see each other once or twice a week and he wanted it to go further. He was so keen that it seemed risky to continue: his enthusiasm made it too likely that word of our encounters might spread, and I wasn't ready for my hometown or family to know just yet.

I probably didn't treat these men fairly or well; my only defence, if it stands as one, is that I had no idea what I was doing. It was still a rollercoaster, and I wasn't always prepared for the steep falls and sudden rises.

For a few weeks, I bounced between Cooranbong and Sydney, learning about the new world while trying to keep things on an even keel in the old one. What I needed after nine months of remarkable change was to take a step back from both.

Absurd good fortune intervened, as it had done so often. Heath was about to start filming a movie in Prague, and Michael suggested I fly over for the shoot. I jumped at the chance. It would be a six-week escape; I'd only need to pay for the airfare and set aside a little spending money, and I'd finally be able to see a little of the world. Apart from one trip to Bali, I'd never been overseas, so I booked my ticket and flew out in September. The film was *The Brothers Grimm*, with Heath starring opposite Matt Damon, but for me it was great just to be back with Michael, who as always found endless amusement on the streets. Armed with a digital camera, he would take photos of anything that caught his eye, from an odd-looking old woman or an eccentric car, to groups of young men who he'd lure into arm-wrestling contests.

We walked from one end of Prague to the other. I was agog at its beauty and the history that seemed to seep from its walls; I'd never been anywhere like it. And socially, I was again thrown into the surreal world of Hollywood on location.

One night I found myself playing pool with Matt Damon, who jokingly reprimanded me for trying to beat him by enforcing what he called *those Aussie rules*. As I'd always found with Heath, he was easy to like and didn't behave as if his fame gave him permission to pull rank. Back home in Australia, friends were scratching their heads at how strange my life could be when I sent them text messages telling them what I was doing: cleaning up Matt Damon at pool in a Prague nightclub on his 33rd birthday. But there was more to the trip than celebrity parties. Being away made me realise how much I needed the break from the upheaval of recent months. Now that Michael and I knew the truth about each other, he was an even more important figure than he'd been before. He was older, and regarded the circus of the Sydney gay scene with an amused but cynical eye.

Bushyyyyyyyyyy! he'd say as I told him this or that story, or relayed one or other of my recent heartaches and dilemmas. He'd draw the last syllable out and shake his head with a gentle, wry smile. The knots I could tie myself in concerned, bemused and amused him, and he didn't need to say much more than that: my nickname, stretched to its limit. We would talk for hours and our conversations were unguarded. All the walls were down. He told me his secrets and I told him mine. Sometimes I wished I could be more like him: older, wiser, less prone to being ambushed by my emotions. And I think he might have sometimes envied me: young, inexperienced, discovering it all for the first time. We drew something from each other, and by the time I left Prague we'd cemented a friendship of total integrity, an unbreakable bond.

I returned to Sydney in mid-October, refreshed and relaxed. I was itching to get back on the rollercoaster I'd stepped off six weeks earlier. As confusing as it could be, it was also great fun, and for the first time I was coming home to a life that felt almost well-rounded. I had friends who *knew* me, friends I had to hide nothing from, and I couldn't wait to see them again.

I went back to work almost immediately, but my weekend habits changed. For years I'd spent every Saturday and Sunday working at home or competing in rodeo or campdraft, but I let that slide and threw myself into a different sort of education. I began spending almost every weekend in Sydney, scooting down the freeway every Saturday night and home again late on Sunday or early Monday morning, staying with a mate in Kings Cross.

In that small and incestuous gay world in Sydney, nobody spoke like me, dressed like me, or did the things I did. People lived in the same area, went to the same gym, the same restaurants, the beaches, the same bars, and I suppose I was unusual. I didn't know much about any of that, and I cared even less. The paradox worked to my advantage and I made friends quickly. My eccentricities even got me noticed by nightclub bouncers, who would wave me through their doors, and waive the exorbitant cover charges, too. Those weekends were the core of my initiation into gay life in Sydney, and they were wonderful. There were long nights of clubbing, and long nights of just talking to my new friends. I'd pour out much of what was in my brain: old fears and new hopes. The year drew to a close and spring turned to summer.

The previous December I'd had the disastrous but pivotal encounter with Jeff under the tree. December 2003 proved just as momentous. One Saturday night at Arq I spotted a young bloke dancing a couple of metres away. I liked him at first sight and summoned the courage to speak to him. We chatted for a while and I told him where I was from and what I did. I gave him my number, and told him to call me sometime. If he was interested, he could come up to my place one weekend and I'd take him for a ride. His name was Chris and he said he'd call. I hoped he meant it.

In the middle of the month, another call came, this time from Michael, who was back in Sydney for the summer. So were Heath and Naomi, as Heath had bought a house in Bronte, around the coast from Bondi on Sydney's eastern beaches, and was settling in there. On New Year's Eve, I was invited to join their celebrations. Early in the night we were at Heath's new home, preparing to go out for dinner, when he said casually: *Bushy, I've just read this script and it sounds a lot like you.*

It was a script about gay cowboys, he explained, and he was weighing up whether to take the leading role. I'd never spoken much to him about Hollywood business, and I didn't this time, either. I just remember thinking it sounded unusual. It also sounded unlikely. Gay cowboys? Who'd want to watch that?

Chapter 18

FOR ALL the changes of the year that had just passed, I was still a cowboy – a horseman with an occasionally surreal life on the side in the big city. During the week, it was all horses, and my business was going well. I was putting into practice all that I'd learned with John Stanton and I'd also started taking trick-riding lessons with an accomplished instructor, Leanne Bruce, and found I had a flair for it. More than that, the sheer charge of pulling off the dramatic stunts was enough to keep me going back every week to learn more. I could soon ride while standing rather than sitting in the saddle, or while hanging off the side with my head a few centimetres from the ground, or while being dragged along behind a cantering horse. These weren't skills in wide demand, but I figured they could come in handy if more movie work came up.

It was all about adding as much as I could to my set of

horse skills, and it was paying off; I rarely had to look for business any more because it was coming to me. That was still the world in which I felt most comfortable and when I finally arranged a date with Chris in early January, that was the world I wanted to show him, away from the gay ghetto, the nightclubs and the distracting buzz of the Sydney scene.

I invited Chris up to Cooranbong, and I was impressed when he said yes. I'd discovered how difficult it could be to dislodge the Sydney set from their inner-city comfort zone, yet Chris didn't hesitate. He spent hours with me in the stables and the yards, watching me work and helping with the horses. It was a small fantasy coming true: that I would find a man who would get in and have a go at whatever needed to be done. He wasn't afraid of getting his hands dirty. More than that, he loved horses, and knew how to ride. He shovelled shit out of stables, fed, watered and brushed my horses, wanted to know everything about the work I was doing. It was easy enough to believe that I could fall in love with someone like this.

Chris met Mum and Dad – again, I just introduced him as a mate, but they must have wondered what was going on. They knew I'd been spending a lot of time in Sydney, and I'd never told them why. This young man I'd invited up was nothing like my typical mates; for all his willingness to step into my life in the country, he had the edge of someone from the city – an attitude, a way of dressing and a way of speaking that marked him as different. I knew I was reaching a critical moment with Mum and Dad. The deception had a shelf life that was very close to expiring, but still I bluffed it. They wondered, but didn't ask. I fretted, but didn't tell.

In the late afternoon, I took Chris for a ride on the beach. That was enough to make it all worth it: me and a man I liked galloping on horseback along the sand at Blackhead Beach. For the first time, I could imagine a life in which every part of me could thrive, the contradictions irrelevant.

After that weekend, we started seeing each other regularly. At times I had to pinch myself: *I had a boyfriend.* It seemed unreal, but as far as I could tell, Chris was as keen as I was. *You're rocking my world,* he told me once in those early weeks, and I was on a high for days. I wanted to tell everyone, because this was real – at last. I told a couple of local friends, and they were accepting and happy for me. My confidence was growing, and it was inevitable who would be next: my family.

Later in January, Mum and Dad went to Tamworth for a week and I decided to have a small party at home while they were away. I invited Chris, Scott and Alex, some Sydney mates and a handful of locals. We had a barbecue at home, then drove to the local pub to meet Leah and Sally, who were there with their boyfriends. My usual defences were down; happiness had knocked them all over, and I didn't care who knew. I was standing alone with Sally and Leah, and without much thought about what I was going to say or what the reaction might be, I said: *I'm gay.*

It was done.

Not even my sisters' initial disbelief and shock could wipe the smile off my face or dampen the relief I felt at having crossed that bridge. I could have chosen a better moment than this, drunk in the local pub where everyone knew me and my family, and where my sisters were robbed of any chance to take it in quietly. We went home soon afterwards, and one of my mates spoke to them, telling them there was no reason to be sad or angry.

The only difference between your brother now and your brother before is that he's a happier man for having told you. He was always gay. The only thing that's changed is that he's accepting it.

Their worries passed quickly. Sally's greatest fear was for Mum and Dad. *They have to know,* she said. Word had spread around the pub, and she was concerned that they would find out through local gossip rather than from me. She was right. They were due back in two days, and I knew I'd have to find the courage to have the most difficult conversation of all.

MANY MOTHERS and fathers imagine that their children trust them above everyone else, and will always turn to them first in times of trouble. They believe that because they've created you, raised you and supported you, there is a bond that overrides every other fear and doubt. But they are the hardest people of all to tell. Parents don't want to learn that they have been lied to, and they don't want to learn that their child has suffered in silence for years rather than seek their understanding and comfort. It's the very depth and strength of the bond that can make coming out so difficult. While a parent can't see it ever breaking, the child wonders if this will be the thing that makes it snap.

I ran through the conversation a thousand times in my head. Part of me felt that surely they would have to see that I was as happy as I'd ever been and, however hard they found it at first, ultimately they would be unable to deny me that. But I dreaded disappointing them. I worried about the loss they would feel, an anxiety made worse by the fact that I was their only son. I feared their anger at my dishonesty: in admitting I was gay, I was confessing to lying – not just once, explicitly, in that conversation with Mum, but over and over again, for years. There had been lies great and small. In the closet you lie every single day, even if you never open your mouth. And at heart, overwhelming every other nagging fear, there is the terror of rejection. You hear of it happening, of young men and women being ejected from the family home, having their lives dismissed and denied by those closest to them. Sometimes religion plays a part; often there is just raw ignorance and lack of understanding, unsupported even by deep faith.

All of these anxieties ran through me as I thought about the conversation to come. I could look back at my life and think of the things I'd done. Contemplating suicide. Prison. Swimming with sharks. The road train. I'd done all that, and now here it was: an ordinary weekday afternoon; the most frightening moment of my life.

Mum, I've got something to tell you.

Mum looked at me.

I'm gay.

The words came out with certainty. They had been there in one way or another for 15 years, for a long time so unformed I couldn't even say them to myself let alone say them out loud. But this time my voice didn't break. I wasn't shaking. Had I known what was going to happen next, they might have remained hidden for a time longer.

Mum was distraught. She cried. She was irrational.

No you're not, she said.

She can laugh at that now, but at the time she didn't know what to say and didn't want to believe it. She was a religious woman who went to Bible studies every week, and I remember she mentioned the Scriptures and told me that it was wrong in God's eyes. Her voice was raised and she was angry as much as she was tearful.

I started crying, and Leah came over to comfort me. But I wasn't about to back away, couldn't back away – I could hardly respond by telling her she was right, and that I had just made it up. Instead, I continued with the truth. I told her I'd met someone, and she guessed straight away that I was talking about Chris.

Then Dad walked into the room.

Adam's got something to tell us. He's gay.

Dad looked as if he didn't know what to say, then told me: *I'd started to think maybe you were.*

He said little after that, while Mum bombarded me with questions, none of them easy to answer. She feared I would get AIDS, believed I would move away and change. Afterwards, I called Leigh to tell her what I'd done, and to ask her to call Mum to talk to her, calm her down. That was among my worst ideas, piling insult upon shock. Someone else, someone close to Mum, had found out before she did.

It could hardly have gone any worse. I'd caused a collision between her religious faith and her loyalty to her son, as well as between her faith in me and the reality of my deception. From her point of view, when she had asked me two years earlier if I was gay she had received a direct and unequivocal answer: *No I'm not. Why would you think that?* And she had taken me at my word.

I was taken aback at the vehemence of her reaction but decided I could only be patient. I told Mum and Dad: *It's taken me years to come to terms with it, I don't expect you to accept it overnight.*

It's a truth often forgotten in the emotion of the moment, but I recognised it: my parents needed time just as I had done.

I went about my work. For all the tension my coming out had caused, I felt vast relief. But things didn't improve quickly. Mum barely spoke to me for days. Dad seemed to have taken it better, but was just keeping his sadness to himself. Leah once heard him sobbing, and said the only time she had heard him cry like that was when a favourite horse had died and he blamed himself for its death. Now he wondered whether to blame himself for this: had he been a bad father, too troubled himself to build a proper relationship with his son? There were regrets and questions. He even worried that something had happened to me in prison, a sexual assault that had made me this way.

I could lay all my father's doubts to rest easily. He had never been anything other than the father I wanted, and I'd never had anything but love and respect for him. Nothing had happened to me in jail. This was just who I was, and I'd known it for years.

Dad also worried about my relationship with Mum, who had taken it so hard she returned to the counsellor who had helped the family after my car accident. I knew Mum well enough to know this couldn't last. We'd always been close and I knew this wasn't her. She was and is the glue of our family, the one who has always held us together, the woman whose strength and determination had helped us through the dark years after Adam Gosden's death. In reacting as she did, shock was playing its part, and there was also an element of responding as she thought she *should* react. Underneath it all, I also knew she carried a parcel of grief for what she thought she was losing – not just the grandchildren I might have given them, or the continuation of the family name, but the very essence of me. She imagined I would leave, that I would change, that I would become a different person.

At our lowest point in those weeks, Mum told me she would not have my gay friends in her house. I told her that if she didn't want gay people in her house, then she surely didn't want me there. I briefly thought about leaving, but she slowly fought her way through her own confusion. One afternoon, we sat down again and talked. Mum told me of her fears and disappointments.

I told her: *Mum, you don't have to worry that I will ever change. I'm never going to change. I'm still me. I'm just happy now.*

We embraced and cried that day, and I think that was the moment Mum made her peace with my sexuality and with me. I never blamed her. It was easier to try to understand. Through all my troubles, she'd always found a way to do that for me.

Chapter 19

I THOUGHT that there were no more hurdles left to cross now that I'd told my family. But then I turned a corner and tripped headlong over a new one. I wasn't prepared for how hard it would be to build and sustain a relationship when one half lived in the country and the other in the city, right in the middle of the gay ghetto.

At first I was on the most sustained emotional high I'd ever experienced. I had a boyfriend. I'd come out to my family, and survived. I was building a wonderful collection of new friends, and as I slowly told some of my older mates, the past and the present seemed to be reconciling in a way that gave me good reason to be optimistic. After years of thinking these two worlds could never live side by side, let alone blend, I was starting to believe that I could make a go of them both without compromising either.

But I was flying blind most of the time. When it came

to relationships, I was clueless, like a teenager finding his first love at high school – and to all intents and purposes, on an emotional level that's exactly where I was. I believed Chris was the one. I desperately wanted it to work, and I was so hungry for the love and affection I'd missed out on that it never occurred to me to go slowly and allow it to develop at its own pace. Now that I had it, I wasn't about to let it go.

Chris was patient. We saw each other every weekend, mostly in Sydney, and I threw myself headlong into his world. Everything he did, I did. His friends became my friends. I wanted to be with him all the time. That meant full immersion in every aspect of gay Sydney, because that was the world he lived in, and when the Mardi Gras festival began in February, my education accelerated so quickly I was dazed by the end of it. There were dance parties, harbour cruises, endless nights in clubs that stayed open until well after sunrise. There were drugs everywhere you turned. Nobody regarded them as dangerous; you'd be more likely to be frowned on for getting drunk, because these parties were devoid of aggro and attitude. I went to them all, then I'd head home exhausted but elated at the end of a weekend and try to focus on my horses – until the following Friday rolled around, and it would start all over again.

Watching from the sidelines, friends would later tell me they were worried: was it all too much, too quickly? They knew how important this, my first relationship, was to me. But was it good for me?

If Chris left, I'd follow. If I didn't know where he was, I'd run off to find him. I thought about him all the time – things I could do for him, things I could give him, places we could go, what our future would hold. I thought that for him to know how I felt about him, I had to show him all the time. One weekend, I arrived on his doorstep in Darlinghurst with a gift: I'd caught a snake in the yard at home, then built a glass tank for it. I knew he was off-the-wall enough to appreciate it; I thought it was the most romantic thing I'd ever done, and the ultimate expression of who I was. Other men might take him to dinner and a movie; I could catch wildlife, and present it to him as a pet.

Chris loved his snake, but his flatmates – two drag queens who performed in the Oxford Street clubs – were less impressed. One afternoon they discovered it had escaped its cage and was loose in their home, and the bedlam that followed as they tried to find it was perhaps the most fitting metaphor for our relationship. Sometimes, country and city are not destined to mix.

I wanted it too badly. Chris didn't want it badly enough. I suspect I would have scared most people away with the pressure of my enthusiasm and expectations. He tried to distance himself, gently at first. Then he'd take longer and longer to return my calls, until eventually he started disappearing from nightclubs, leaving me there alone. I copped it all, then kept coming back for more. In the end, four months after we met, he was forced to be harsh: I was dumped. Looking back, I don't blame him. I don't think anyone could have delivered all that I wanted at that time, because the hole I was trying to fill was simply too large. It took me some time to realise that, and to understand that I'd learned my most important lesson yet about love: how to endure the broken heart that's left when it doesn't work out.

I WAS exhausted, and once I'd battled my way past the sadness, I was confused. In its own way, coming out was like getting out of prison: facing decisions I'd never had to make, weighing choices that had never existed, trying to find my way in a world that had changed completely. I threw myself into the things I'd neglected – my work, friendships, family – but still felt that familiar gnawing feeling that I knew meant only one thing: I needed to get away.

Heath had signed to *Brokeback Mountain* – the film about gay cowboys he had mentioned to me on New Year's Eve – and they would be filming in Canada during the Australian winter. Michael asked if I wanted to come over and visit. He even thought I might be able to pick up some work on the set, given the extensive use of horses in the script. That put the idea in my head, but the film work didn't sound very certain and I wanted to take myself away for longer than a few weeks.

In the end one phone call resolved it. Over the years I'd been in sporadic contact with Lynne Chassion, who'd dated

Ken in Cairns while I was working on the prawn trawlers 10 years earlier – the woman I'd written to, and come closest to confiding in at a time when I talked to no one. The funny thing was that a decade later, she still didn't know the whole truth. She'd moved back to Canada and was living in Moosejaw, a small town in Saskatchewan. I called her and said I was thinking of coming to visit. She had friends with a large property and she thought I'd probably be able to get some horse work with them. Nothing was set in stone, but nothing with me ever had been. In late June, I was on a plane to Calgary.

Michael and Heath picked me up at the airport and as we drove into the city I was immediately glad I'd made the trip. The Calgary Stampede was on that weekend, and I was more excited about that than about visiting the film set. The Stampede was legendary: the world's largest rodeo event, held over 10 days and attracting more than a million people every year. It consumes the entire city, which looks to have been taken over by cowboys. I couldn't have felt more at home. We went to the main arena that night – Michael, myself and his musician mate from Los Angeles, Doug – and watched the spectacle first-hand. The next day, it was cowboys again – this time on the set of *Brokeback Mountain*.

I'd left it too late in the shoot to score any work, but it was thrill enough to be back with Michael and Heath and to see the final weeks of filming unfold. It was all but a closed set, I think mainly because early in filming a paparazzi photographer had managed to snap a shot of stunt doubles for Heath and Jake Gyllenhaal during a scene in which they jumped naked off a ledge into a river. The image had ended up in the tabloids and the producers weren't taking any more chances. I was lucky they let me near the set at all.

What struck me was what a small and tight-knit crew this was, far smaller than I'd experienced on *Ned Kelly* or *The Brothers Grimm* in Prague. It seemed to fit with the kind of intimate film they were making, though I didn't know much about it even then. I remember Heath taking a break from filming one afternoon and sitting down on the grass for a chat. It had been a long, demanding shoot and he was tired, looking forward to it finishing soon. It was no surprise he was drained. Even taking the role had been a gamble, and I knew he would have given it his all. It was the kind of role and film he loved – edgy, out of the mainstream – and he'd always struck me as an actor who wanted to do difficult work. The celebrity side of the business was not for him; he was not in the thrall of money and fame and box office figures. The word was that he was turning in a good, perhaps truly great, performance. But he was innately modest, and the film was far too risky and unusual for anyone involved to start counting chickens yet.

Away from the set, I heard little discussion about it. Instead it was the social whirl I was now familiar with whenever I spent time with them: dinners, bars, parties, casual nights at home. I spent a lot of time with Michael and Doug.

Doug was a friendly giant of a man and we fell into an easy friendship. When shooting finished, the director Ang Lee hosted the wrap party at a restaurant in Calgary. I felt a little out of place, having had nothing to do with the film, but was made welcome, and my memory of the night is of the heart-felt speeches recognising the achievement of the cast and crew. It was a low-key and humble affair. It seemed to me that they knew then that they had made something special, but no one was daring yet to imagine just how far-reaching the impact would be.

Heath and Michael had to return to LA. I had to get to Moosejaw, but first came an offer too hard to knock back. Heath had a lot of stuff he needed to get back to his home in California, from things he'd bought during the shoot and souvenirs from the set to his beloved Harley, which he'd brought with him so he could unwind with rides on the country roads when he wasn't filming. He asked Doug and me if we felt like a road trip: he'd hire a small van, we could load it with all his gear and drive it back to LA for him. All expenses paid. There was nothing to think about; we jumped at the idea.

We stashed the motorcycle and other gear into a U-Haul trailer and hit the road. We had 10 days to get to LA; what we did in the meantime was up to us, and we made the most of it. The route south was enticing: there were four beautiful American states between us and California, and much of it really was *Brokeback* territory – the Big Sky states of Montana and Wyoming, where much of Annie Proulx's original short story was set, then down through Utah and into Nevada. These were landscapes unlike any I'd ever seen at home, soaring mountains and endless prairies. Doug and I would stop to fish in ice-cold streams, or park off in small towns where he would raid the local antique stores and come away with bargains that we'd add to the load in our truck.

When we got to Vegas, our journey shifted from the sublime to the ridiculous. There is nothing subtle or calming about the place, but it jolts your senses as severely as any stunning snow-covered landscape. We checked into the Mandalay Bay resort, and Doug used his music-industry contacts to get us tickets to a show that night, complete with backstage passes. A few days later, I crossed the border into another place that feels like another world: California, so familiar you feel like you know it even if you've never set foot there.

Heath lived in a Spanish villa in the Hollywood Hills and that was our first stop. We off-loaded his bike and other gear, then made for Michael's home in Venice Beach. This was as far from Cooranbong as could be, a trendy beachside strip where the sand was jammed with bodybuilders and models and everyone seemed to have perfect teeth and a flawless tan. Yet for all its superficiality, it still oozed character and eccentricity. You felt as if you could be anyone and do anything, and no one would bat an eye. Even a gay cowboy didn't feel out of place, but I couldn't linger long. I was already late getting back to the real world. I had to fly to Moosejaw.

Lynne and I had not seen each other for years, and on the first night I had to do something I'd quickly become used to: come out. There always seemed to be someone new to tell. Lynne was, as I'd expected, happy for me and delighted that I'd made my peace. For me it was a relief just to be away, in a place I didn't know and with an old friend to talk to. I'd gone to Canada unsure how long I'd be away, but soon realised I'd be happy to stay there as long as I could.

Things fell into place in a hurry. Lynne introduced me to her friends and they agreed to take me on to train some horses, so within days I had both a home and an income. I was instantly comfortable there; Canadians struck me as being more similar to Australians than the Americans I'd known. They were more laid-back, and just as attached to their dry sense of humour. To them, I was a novelty. Moosejaw has a population of about 30,000 people, and unsurprisingly I was the only Australian among them. There was a strange kind of comfort in just being me, and letting my mind slow down after 18 months of it spinning at a dizzying pace. I was just the Aussie cowboy, doing what I loved, and it was good to ground myself in that old identity and rediscover its familiar rhythms of early mornings and hours outdoors that ended in tired satisfaction after a day's labour.

*

MOOSEJAW COULD feel like it was a long way from anywhere, but these days nowhere is isolated. Lynne's computer, and the same gay website that I'd used in Sydney, showed me that.

I'd used the website occasionally in Canada to stay in touch with friends back home – it gave me instant contact and live conversation without the expense of a phone call – but I also discovered I could relocate myself in the virtual world and drop myself into whatever community on the planet I happened to be in. I didn't expect to find anyone in Moosejaw, but Regina, the capital of Saskatchewan, was only a 45-minute drive away and with a population of a quarter of a million I figured there would have to be someone to talk to.

That was how I met Justin, three months after I arrived. He was, in a very classic sense, tall, dark and handsome: 23, six feet four, well-built and *smart* – book smart, something I'd never been. He was a medical student who lived with his parents and earned cash to fund studies and a social life by making coffees at a local Starbucks. In other words, other than remaining in the family home we had absolutely nothing in common. But given where I was I figured I couldn't expect the matchmaking to be perfect. We arranged to meet at a bar in Regina. I didn't take it too seriously, even turning up for the date with friends in tow.

I'd never met anyone quite like Justin – young, serious, inclined to intellectual conversation – and he'd never met anyone like me – young, frivolous, inclined to joke and lark.

Within minutes of meeting him, I'd taken his cap off and told him he looked silly in it. It took him a while to realise that I spent much of my time taking the mickey. It was an unlikely beginning, and at the time I didn't even think of it as one. You don't often get a warning that you're about to fall in love.

I'll never understand why Justin kept coming back for more – then and later – but he did. Our first date consisted of nothing more than a kiss, but we met again, then again, and soon we were sleeping together. I'd never experienced anything like it. I could see on reflection that my relationship with Chris had been driven largely by me, because I was so keen he never had much reason to worry about pushing it forward himself. With Justin, the roles were reversed: he fell quickly and heavily, and inundated me with love and attention. I'd never had it before and was only too ready to lap it up. I didn't have to do anything; he was just there whenever he could be, telling me I was wonderful and even daring to talk about a future together. I was flattered, and floored. By the time things started getting serious, I was close to leaving Moosejaw, but it was obvious this was something I could not just leave behind. We made plans for him to come to Australia in February; if that worked, we would consider how we might make it more permanent.

I flew first to London for a three-week break, then home – back to work, and to wait for Justin.

Chapter 20

I WAS pleased to be home and happy I did not have long to wait until Justin arrived. It was early December, traditionally a time for taking stock. For me, December had often been the month of events and decisions: my car accident, leaving for Scone, leaving some to start my business, my encounter with Jeff, meeting Chris in Sydney. This year, I was thinking of little else but Justin. Could I make it work with this Canadian?

The test would be that this time he would be in my world. It was confronting for me that he would be the first man I'd openly brought home as a partner since I came out a year earlier. Where would he sleep? Would Mum and Dad cope? Would they like him? Would my friends like him? I was nervous for him as much as for me, and looking back I think I was also terrified of losing face. I'd told everyone about him. I'd painted him as the likely key to my future. There was the big question: had I put too much pressure on us both, and set us and everyone else up for disappointment?

It turned out to be a month of ups and downs. Michael was back in Sydney for the summer, and had a twinkle in his eye from the moment he met my freshly imported boyfriend. *Nice tan*, was the first thing he said to the pale Canadian who'd arrived fresh from the depths of winter. Michael then christened him *Bushy's Bride*. But it was not going to be a smooth road to relationship bliss: Justin struggled from the start to fit in. The Sydney party scene, at its height in January, was not for him. Days on the beach were a challenge: he'd lived his life in the centre of cold Canada, and was not a good swimmer. On first meeting, he could come across as a little stiff and difficult to talk to, because of his tendency to launch without warning into a serious conversation or to quote from a book he'd once read. Justin was also a gym nut and would ask me to take him home from the pub so he could have dinner and a good night's sleep; he didn't want to break his exercise routine just because he was on holiday. Friends wondered: could I really be happy with someone who made me leave the pub after just two beers? He battled to warm to my friends and they struggled to warm to him.

It pained me, because I understood why they found Justin hard to relate to, and could see what they meant when they said there were too many differences, that he was just not the right man for me. Mum and Dad were generous, as they had always been with any person who entered the family home. Mum, reluctantly at first, gave her blessing for us to share a bed: she accepted me, she said, and could not treat me any differently to my sisters when their partners stayed over. When they met him they liked him, but like everyone they sensed he was probably not the one for me. I could feel the judgements from outside, even when they weren't openly expressed. But I also knew that I was falling for him and that whatever he was, Justin loved me.

Justin was as fundamentally generous and decent a man as I could ever hope to find. He would never tire of telling me how proud he was to have me by his side, and how much he wanted us to plan a future together. But in feeling how much he loved me, I also felt smothered at times. After three weeks, two nights before he was due to go home, we had a blistering fight. The trigger was an incident with some friends of mine – I thought he'd been rude to them – but it was sparked by something deeper. I was feeling the pressure of his looming departure, and was unsure what to do next. He was certain what he wanted; my friends and family were equally certain about what they thought was best. What did I want? I had no idea, but I was being pelted from all sides and from within, and it came out as rage.

It almost ended right there, but something brought me back from the brink. I apologised the next day and told Justin I wanted to carry on. He was already talking about moving to Australia to be with me and continue his studies. I put him on the plane with a promise that we would stay committed to each other; I would go back to Canada in the middle of the year and we could take stock then.

A kind of calm descended then, the first real stretch of routine and normality I'd had in two years. I made work my priority, with occasional weekend trips to Sydney to see friends. Justin and I spoke often, but the more time I had to think, the more unlikely it seemed that we could make a go of it. The commitment of time and money involved in one of us moving to another country permanently was enormous. I was still not convinced I was ready for it, or that I could in good conscience ask it of him.

I flew to Canada on 4 July. I reasoned that I couldn't make the right decision while we were so far apart, and nor could he. He met me at the airport, and from the first moment there was never a doubt that he remained besotted. That made me even more uncertain, because I doubted I could ever match the depth of his feeling. There were times I treated him harshly, just as Chris had once done to me. I'd push him away, refuse to see him, rebuff his affection. It was like looking in a mirror: *the hole he was trying to fill was simply too large*. But he kept coming back for more, as I had once done. That persistence began to batter down my defences, and with time I came to see that I *did* love him. I even told him so. The nagging doubt was whether I loved him enough.

In the end I knew only one thing for certain: that I wasn't ready to walk away from him yet. That was hardly a ringing endorsement of our relationship, and perhaps it would have been kinder to set out my doubts more explicitly. Instead, I once more held out the teasing prospect of a future together. I asked him to come to Australia again at Christmas. The best I can say for the invitation was that while it did not feel exactly right, nor did it feel all wrong. I *was* in love with him. With that as my starting point, I hoped the rest would come naturally.

It didn't, of course. That I ever held the hope shows just how little I still understood matters of the heart. I was in love with the *idea* of being in love. And I loved to be loved as much as Justin loved me. But no relationship could ever fly with wings as clipped as mine were when I was with him. I harboured too many doubts, recognised too many differences and fretted over too many obstacles to let myself go completely.

Justin arrived a few days before Christmas. Nothing had changed for him. I remained the man he wanted to be with, the man he would do anything for. I'd open the door, then slam it again, then open it once more. I could hardly blame him for not knowing what to think or do. There were moments of intense connection and enjoyment, but I knew I was deceiving him and fooling myself. If we were meant to be together, this was not the time. I finally found the courage to tell him so.

One day it might work. Just not now.

It was all I could offer. Justin didn't want to accept it,

but I put him on the plane, telling myself it was over. His heart was broken, and for all I'd done wrong I had at least come far enough to know exactly how he felt. To have now been on both sides of that pain was an education in itself.

Chapter 21

LOVE – THE word said out loud, or just the idea of it rumbling around in my head – could hypnotise me. It seems to be one of the crueller punishments of years in the closet that once you've stepped out and finally opened yourself to feeling something, you're not sure how to recognise it or what to do with it. I had no idea how to show love in return, how to accept it or find the courage to turn it away, how to recognise its opportunities, how to live with its limitations. Justin loved me and never stopped telling me so, and it was that knowledge that attracted and repelled me at the same time. It could overwhelm me at times – it was what I'd been craving all those years, and it sometimes amazed me to think that anyone could feel that way about *me*. But was it enough? Could I give it back – and if I could, was *that* enough?

You grow up believing that love is everything, but I was

discovering far too late in life that it's not that simple. I'd never been allowed, or allowed myself, to learn these lessons when I was growing up, as I probably would have done if I'd been straight. In my early thirties, I was facing a rapid education.

I couldn't shake the nagging doubt that I might have made a mistake. That was another lesson: as a mate told me, love and doubt walk around together more often than love and certainty. I threw myself back into work, and as always being with the horses brought me a certain peace – as the cowboy, I was in charge. But I was also realising that in many ways it had held me back. I was living my dream – had taken my passion and made a life from it – but had not quite shaken the feeling that these two parts of me, the cowboy and the gay man, were not supposed to live side by side. Even if I could accommodate them, there were plenty of reasons to wonder if the rest of the world could accept them in one package. And I understood why, because my own judgements had been swayed by the stereotypes as much as anyone's.

By early 2006, two years had passed since I'd told my family and I assumed most people around home knew. The country gossip network would have taken care of that and I was happy enough to leave it to the bush telegraph, because it saved me having to come out to friends and clients and relatives over and over again. I never felt any kind of backlash or rejection, at least not to my face – but occasionally would hear a story that pulled me up short. James, a 17-year-old who worked for me regularly, once told me that his young mates had given him a hard time because he was working with *Adam the poofter* and another mate said he'd leapt to my defence when he heard some local lads bagging me. I tried not to let those stories get to me – I knew better than anyone how novel the idea of the gay cowboy was. Whatever my doubts, I'd come far enough to know that this *was* me, and that I would have to slowly settle into my own skin and leave the stereotypes behind.

I wasn't the only one who faced that battle. A week after Justin left, it was the Australia Day long weekend in late January, and Craig Swain, my cattle farmer mate out Tamworth way, was taking his own big step forward. He was having his 30th birthday party, but it was a more important event than that. He'd long wanted to bring all his worlds together – his family, his country friends, his gay mates from the bush and the city – and he'd decided this was the moment. It was also the test: would it work?

We all gathered on Craig's property near Tamworth on a searingly hot weekend, a long way from Oxford Street – there were cowboy hats, bales of hay, kegs of beer, utes, horses, cattle dogs, a mechanical bull, dance music, farmers' wives, straight men, gay men, couples with children – even gay couples with children. The worlds collided, and didn't break.

Craig's dad, a fifth-generation farmer whose family

had been on the land in the area for more than a century, made a speech telling of his pride in his son, and welcoming Craig's partner, Mark, to the fold. Then he welcomed all of us, too, and said how happy he was that we were there to celebrate.

Craig spoke next, and embraced his life – all of it – in front of everyone he cared about. He said this had been his dream, to bring his two halves together, and then he did what not too many men had done in his circumstances – he spoke of his romance with another man, and said with pride to his partner, in front of dozens of people standing in a paddock: *Mark, I love you, mate.*

That same weekend, the private journey of men like Craig and me was finding a much wider audience. *Brokeback Mountain* was released on Australia Day, 26 January, though people had been talking about it for a long time before it hit the cinemas. It was released in the US in December and was more than an unexpected box office success – it was also a film the media were describing as a landmark for Hollywood, for gay people, and particularly for Heath. One newspaper compared him to Marlon Brando, and there was a lot of talk that his performance would win him an Oscar. Like most gay men, I couldn't wait to see it, but I approached it with more complicated feelings than most. There was simple curiosity, because I'd been on the set and wanted to see how the finished film had turned out, and there was personal interest, because some of the people named in the credits, from actors to set painters, were mates. And then there was more profound curiosity. I remembered the conversation on New Year's Eve two years before. *Bushy, I've just read this script and it sounds a lot like you.*

When I saw the film I found it gut-wrenching. There was a lot of me in the movie, but it wasn't there because of anything Heath had taken from knowing me. Most gay men, especially most country gay men, seemed to find something of themselves in the story, and those truths had been there long before it was a film and before Heath was asked to play Ennis del Mar. Later, I heard a comment by Annie Proulx, who had written the original short story 10 years earlier. She said that the inspiration for it came one night in a bar in Wyoming, when she saw an older man watching some young men playing pool. He had *a kind of bitter longing, that made me wonder if he was country gay*. I knew what she meant. Country gay was different. Cowboy gay was different. No one had ever really bothered to examine how and why before, but she'd done it, and then Heath had brought it to life on screen.

Heath didn't seem to be doing much. Everything was held inside, and all the pain was in his eyes. There is one scene where Ennis asks Jack, his secret cowboy lover, if sometimes he feels like people know, just by looking. I'd often had that feeling, that I was somehow betraying the truth through my eyes. All that fear and anger and denial was on the screen, and churned inside me while I watched it. In another scene,

Ennis flies into a sudden rage on a street, and I knew that I'd been there, too, angry beyond measure without obvious reason. Throughout the film he swings from the relief and pleasure of finally being himself to the hatred and terror when he thinks about it afterwards. He hurts everyone he loves and shuts them out, and at one point he tells Jack that they are not allowed to be like this. *Two guys living together,* he says. *No way*. They might end up dead.

When Jack Twist does die, Ennis imagines the love of his life has been killed in a gay bashing, which brought back one of my worst memories – the night I woke in a street in Cairns, beaten to a pulp. I wondered, is that what happened to me? By the end of the film I was shattered. It was surreal, because I'd been on set when they shot the final scene, and all these months later I was watching it again, but this time my stomach was in a knot.

It's hard to explain why it affected me and other gay men so deeply – some straight people said they didn't get what all the fuss was about. When I saw it in the cinema I even heard nervous giggles and groans at moments I found the most moving and powerful. In a way those reactions showed how important the film was, because people were seeing a depiction of emotions and circumstances they hadn't been confronted with before. If it made them uneasy, it might also have made them think – and by the end, no one was sniggering.

For men who'd lived lives like mine, the film was

important for another simple reason. Most people – straight people – find bits of themselves, their experiences and their feelings, in movies, books and songs their whole lives. I'd always loved old Hollywood westerns, and the dry, rough-and-tumble cowboys in them. But those cowboys didn't feel much, and if they did you had to guess what it might be. In *Brokeback,* the cowboys cried, but only when no one was looking. I was 31, and seeing my reflection for the first time.

The film stayed with me for hours and days afterwards. I went home that night and sat up for hours talking with a mate, and much came flooding out – memories and feelings I hadn't expressed in years. Some I'd never really expressed at all. I was surprised at how intensely the film had taken me back to my own mountain and one of the hardest moments of my life: sitting on that ledge when I was 19, ready to kill myself. Hardly a soul knew about it, and I hadn't thought about it often in recent years. *Brokeback* reminded me of the despair that hatred and loneliness can drive you to. It was brilliant fiction. But it showed there were many true stories that were also worth telling, and this was the moment to tell them.

A FEW days later I heard Bob Katter, a conservative politician from Queensland, talking about *Brokeback* and gay cowboys. *Maybe there are some out there but I've never heard of 'em. I mean, it's not a profession that attracts those sort of people.* When I heard him on the radio I thought: *Hang on, there's one right here*. I knew a journalist, and he believed I had the story, so then I had the opportunity. I took it, though not before fighting off many fears and doubts. Going public was a terrifying decision in many ways, but I held my nerve and went ahead with it.

Then the day came, and nothing could have prepared me for it. It was Saturday 4 March. The timing was deliberate. The Oscars were two days away and Heath was one of the favourites to win Best Actor. By coincidence, it was also the day of the Mardi Gras parade and party, the biggest events on Sydney's gay calendar. This was the moment in time, and there it was that morning: *Meet Heath's mate, the real gay cowboy.*

The headline ran across the top of the front page of the *Sydney Morning Herald*, above a photograph of Archie lying on the ground, his head resting in my lap, me nuzzling him and smiling. It had been taken a week earlier in the place that had always meant the most to me, in a clearing on the mountain where I'd gone to kill myself. The article covered that ground, and everything else: the accident, prison, years of roaming, *Ned Kelly*, Michael and Heath. Dad read it and cried. *There are things in there about you that I didn't know,* he said.

For the first time he learned how close I'd come to killing myself. The same was true for many people. There were friends who'd never known about the accident; few knew of the suicide plan; I don't think anyone was prepared for me to lay bare just how much pain I'd been through. The phone started that morning and didn't stop. People began reading the article and finished in tears. I stayed at home all that day, determined to lie low. I didn't want to go Sydney. I was trying to come to terms with what I'd done and the impact it seemed to be having, and the idea of showing my face in the city on the same day that it decorated the front page of newspapers in every corner store was too much to face. And the Mardi Gras parade was on. It would be filled with men paying homage to *Brokeback*, nearly all of them city boys in costume.

I decided this gay cowboy was better off staying home, getting dusty in the yard with his horses. Someone asked me how I felt that day, and I could only use the same words I'd said to Leigh when I came out to her three years earlier: *I feel taller now.*

Soon after the newspaper story appeared, I was contacted by *Australian Story*, a documentary program on the ABC. They wanted to do an episode on my life, and after some thought I agreed. Mum had reservations, as it would involve the whole family and be much more confronting: it was television, and the whole country would see it.

Mum, Dad and I sat down one afternoon to talk it through, and though I hadn't planned it, it turned into the most important conversation we'd ever had. I told Mum that I wanted to do it, and that I'd realised I had an opportunity few people would ever have: to tell my story to the world, and have it make a difference. I said she shouldn't assume it was easy, because it wasn't, but little in my life had been. I'd come through it all by taking chances, by being brave, and by following my instincts. More importantly, I'd come through it all because of them and all they had given me. *You have always been there for me through the good and the bad, giving me strength. I am who I am because of you. I want you to know that without you I would not be the man I am today,* I said.

The tears came to Mum first, then to me, then to Dad. She stood, came over and hugged me and held me tight, telling me that she loved me and would support me in whatever I wanted to do. Then Dad hugged me, and I knew that if nothing else came of it all, my family had crossed a bridge. For the first time, I'd found the words to tell Mum and Dad everything they meant to me, and to thank them for everything they'd done. It was the moment I let them in properly for the first time, the end of all the years of lying to them, hurting them and pushing them away. It had been a long time coming.

THE PHONE started ringing the second the broadcast of *Since Adam Was A Boy* ended. There were relatives and friends, of course, but also strangers – men and women from around Australia who had dug our number from the phone book and called to express their appreciation and thanks. Some were in tears. Over the following weeks, the letters and emails flooded in by the score, eventually numbering in the hundreds. There were young gay men from the bush who'd never told a soul, but now thought they'd found the courage, and mothers and fathers who wrote to say they'd drawn strength and understanding from my parents and learned how to accept their own children. The saddest letters were from old men who'd kept the secret all their lives, and understood the pain. They were always generous, often saying thank you for representing their lives, and telling me they were glad I'd found a way out rather than suffer their lifetime of loneliness. There was one from a man my own age, another country boy, that affected me deeply.

It was almost like someone telling the story of my own life, except that you've come out the other end and are living a life that is truly you. I am still stuck in the pretence of being someone else. You said that your horses were the only ones to know the real you. Well, my dogs are the only ones I've told. It seems so dumb to actually say that, but the pressures of being the straight guy are incredibly strong in the bush, as you are more than aware. Mostly these days I've thrown myself into the farm, trying to avoid people really. But when I saw how together you were it gave me a spark of hope that maybe with the support of some people who really understand what it was like to be me that I may some day enjoy that same freedom. I really didn't ever think there were gay guys out there like me.

Things are getting pretty lonely out here and if I don't change things it's going to stay that way. You start questioning the friendships you have when you're in our position and I strongly feel my friends wouldn't really be friends if I told them about me. It's a terrible feeling to really acknowledge that. I even sometimes wonder how conditional my family's love for me is? I'm sorry to crap on like this, but that's most of it out. Even though we're not actually talking it's a relief that the only time I've actually said all of this stuff is to someone who understands. It would mean more than you know if you could possibly write back.

I did write to him. That letter was me, 10 years earlier, completely alone and seeking comfort from a stranger I thought might understand.

IN THE middle of it all, the rhythms of family life carried on. Sally got married in March to her partner of three years, Ben Wrigley, and it was a day that summoned enough emotion all on its own. Leah was a bridesmaid; I drove the bride to church. The three of us had always been close – you only had to watch us have a blue to understand how close we were, because we could rouse at each other as siblings can only do when they know their bond is so strong there will never be a lasting consequence.

Mum and Dad had reason to be proud, not because of anything in particular we'd done as individuals, but because they had raised three happy and healthy kids who loved them, loved each other and who had stood together through good times and bad. On Sally's wedding day, we could stand together as a family and know we were unbreakable.

It was a particularly emotional day for me, watching my little sister walk down the aisle. We'd been through a lot, and I'd never forgotten how loyal Sal had remained through the awful year after my accident. I was young enough then, but she was only 17, yet her letters came weekly, endlessly supportive. Twelve years later, on what was *her* special day, she could still be generous of spirit. She thanked all the important people in her life, and brought herself and me to tears when she told the guests *how proud I am to have you as my big brother. You've taught me a lot about just being yourself.*

But it seemed to me, as I looked at my family that day, that it was they who had taught me – or at least given me all the time and space I needed to learn. Courage and self-acceptance had been a long time coming. I'd never have found them without their patience and understanding at every turn, without them standing behind me. The attention was pretty constant by then – whether it was in letters, emails and phone calls, strangers on the street when I went to Sydney or from the guests at Sally's wedding – and it unnerved me more than I let on. It was flattering, humbling, sometimes confusing.

Later that night, I cried quietly outside in the dark when only one friend was there to see me, and wondered out loud: *why is this happening to me?* I knew better than anyone how scared and uncertain I still was, and how much growing I still had in front of me.

There's nothing special about me, I said.

Maybe that's the point, my friend said.

They were far from the only tears to fall that day. Dad's tears started as he stood with his daughter on his arm, waiting to enter the church. In the days before the wedding, he'd stopped to reflect. It was funny, he said. He'd always imagined as we grew up that it would be his son, the eldest child, who would get married first. He'd had to come to terms with much more than simply a rearrangement in the expected order of his children's marriages, and he'd accepted it all with grace and courage. They all had. If the public response was overwhelming, it paled to nothing when we recognised that the most important effect went beyond the comfort our family's story had given others. It was this: by telling it, we'd healed ourselves.

We'd been forced to talk and to confront things we'd otherwise have left buried. Dad realised there were things about his son that he didn't know or understand. There was so much he'd been able only to wonder about, and sometimes the wondering had been painful. He told me that when I was in prison, he'd lie awake at night and try to picture me in his head. He'd wonder what I'd done that day, what I was doing then, and hope that I was safe. He'd been through too many nights of wondering and not knowing.

Dad had always been my inspiration, from the moment he first took me fishing on Sydney Harbour as a kid. But as I grew older, I'd felt I could never measure up, because who I *really* was made me less of a man. I found it hard to show him love. A hug was confronting, and the truth was more terrifying than that. Then we told it to each other, and discovered that the truth can't hurt you. After that a hug was easy, and on Sally's wedding day there were many. Dad gave away his daughter, but he'd finally got his son back. And this time, he knew who his son really was.

Epilogue

I'M BACK with the brumbies now, camping out, sleeping in my swag, cooking on a fire, the wild horses nearby. I'm happy that I still have these things to ground me, and that I can still have the stars as my roof and let them do what they do best: make us wonder. I've finished telling my story, but the ending is difficult because it's such a long way from being complete. I've written about the past, which has brought me to where I am. I don't know what the future holds, but I know not to plan too carefully. Enough has happened to teach me that.

It is 12 years since Dad sat in a courtroom and tried to convince a judge to spare me a prison sentence. Now he is talking about me again, trying to explain me to other people, and perhaps trying to explain me to himself. This time he is on television, and there are a million judges.

Dad says: *There's a lot of regret I feel that he had to lie. I wish I'd been there for him more often in his adolescent years to help him through his troubled times. Give him somebody to talk to. Give him somebody to communicate with. I find more love from him now than I did then. And I only wish that I could have been around him more often.*

I say, my voice breaking: *Dad is an inspiration to me. Without his help, without him in my life, I couldn't do what I do. I couldn't do it. There are no words I can put on that man.*

We both have regrets, about things we've done and things we haven't done. We both have lived through mourning, guilt and pain, and still do. When Adam Gosden died, Dad was forced to confront his own demons so he could help me deal with mine. He went to counselling, and for the first time unburdened himself about the war. Why had his mates died and not him? We see where our paths could have been different – if he had never gone to war, if I had never had my accident. We can ask these questions now. When Dad came back, what if my mother had not been waiting? Dad knows what he would have done: run away, as I did after prison. And what if I'd been able to love someone and be loved back when I encountered tragedy? If there had been someone there for me, as Mum was there for Dad, would it have saved me all the hard years to come?

I know now, as Dad does, that it's pointless wondering. You could go mad. We've made what peace we can with the past, and know that we're better able to continue along the rest of that road to reconciliation with ourselves and with others. It will never really end.

I am asked, do I wish I'd never been through all the pain, and had lived only easy days, never hard ones? I know the answer. I can't wish it all away without wishing myself away. I am who I am because of it all.

So I say: *No. You have to accept the lot.*

That's what makes it your life.

Acknowledgments

ADAM'S LIFE story has been told in three stages – in a newspaper, then on television, and now in this book – with each stage revealing new dimensions. Over the past year there have been many people who have helped us discover those added layers, and made it easier in countless ways for us to bring his journey to life in these pages.

In its first incarnation, as a story in *The Sydney Morning Herald*, we were blessed firstly to be accompanied by a remarkable photograph taken by Steven Siewert. Steven's beautiful, evocative image – which now graces the cover of this book – was worth more than the proverbial thousand words; it stands alone as a small masterpiece, and was recognised as such by the judges of the 2006 Walkley Awards, who named it Portrait of the Year. Others among Neil's colleagues at the *Herald* deserve thanks. Amanda Wilson, then the Saturday editor, recognised the power of Adam's story immediately it was told to her, and then made sure it was handled sensitively and displayed beautifully. Deputy night editor Kate Benson, the first person to read the original story, calmed our nerves and let us know we had something special by revealing she was in tears before the end. Rick Feneley, the *Herald*'s genius night editor, shepherded the yarn from raw copy to front page and rang five minutes before deadline to make sure he had a headline that did justice to what he called *this man's heroic journey* – those were lovely words, and Rick later read some early chapters and offered typically savvy advice and encouragement. Alan Oakley, the *Herald*'s editor, deputy editor Mick Millett, news editor Darren Goodsir and chief-of-staff Sean Nicholls, were generous beyond measure in giving Neil the time to pursue this project to its completion.

Adam's story then became a television program – an episode of the ABC's *Australian Story*, called *Since Adam Was A Boy*. The producer, Helen Grasswill, and Ian Hurley, who helped produce the show and later performed visual miracles with his editing, found moments of power and truth in Adam's life that later informed the writing of this book, particularly in their recognition that, at heart, this was a story about a father and his son. This would not be the same book without us having witnessed their beautiful, sensitive telling of the story in another medium.

There was more inspiration to come, this time in a phone call from Di Morrissey, the Australian author, who was so moved by Adam's story after reading the *Herald* that she tracked us down and insisted: *This has to become a book.* Her confidence and belief in the project was pivotal.

Our agent, Lyn Tranter, and her assistant, Wenona Byrne, from Australian Literary Management, loved Adam's story and guided two novices through the minefield of dealing with publishing houses, growing some grey hairs on our behalf. They have never been more than a supportive phone call away. Jane Palfreyman, from Random House, brought integrity, passion and enthusiasm to the table from the start; she trusted us, and we have written a better book because she did so. She has since departed, but her successor, Meredith Curnow, has been a similar joy to deal with. Vanessa Mickan did a superb editing job, making for a much better book. And Sophie Ambrose has been an endless source of quiet passion, encouragement, enthusiasm and patience as she has carried *Say It Out Loud* from raw manuscript to the book you hold now.

On a personal level, we have been fortunate to have the support of two wonderful families and many generous friends. The first words of this book were written in front of an open fire in Bunnerong Cottage at Illawambra, a historic property at Cobargo, where there are rolling hills, horses, dogs, wombats and birds, but no mobile phone coverage – perfect peace. The setting was all the inspiration we needed, and we thank Jenny and Paul Stock for the generous use of the cottage and their encouragement as we faced the terror of the first blank page. In Broome, Ken and Jodie Rockley put us up for two weeks as Adam revisited an old stamping ground and taught Neil about Broometime, and how to waste an entire day on Cable Beach, waiting for the sun to set. We called that research. In Cooranbong, Charlie McAskill saved us by stepping in to do some key research that became integral to the book. Leigh Maule was a devoted friend and supporter from the start, and helped convince us we were on the right track when those moments of doubt set in. Leigh's sister Brooke Stevens, at just 16, sketched the beautiful replica of the cover image as a gift for Adam, and it now finds a home inside the front cover. In Nundle, Craig Swain showed what he's made of by letting us use parts of his story to help illuminate Adam's own. Further afield – in Moosejaw, Canada – Lynne Chassion rummaged through boxes to find some old letters that provided a unique window into Adam's past.

Finally, our families. Neil's parents, Bill and Julie, and sister Caroline, have never been less than 100 per cent supportive from the beginning, a truth that has held true for 20 years as a sometimes unusual life and career have unfolded. They have always given me my head, and most of the time I've found a way to use it wisely. They make everything easier.

Adam's family – John and Barb; Sally, Ben and Coby; Leah – have been intimately involved in this project from the beginning. It is difficult to find words to reflect their courage. At every turn, when it would have been easier to say *No* or to turn the other way, they have instead chosen *Yes,* and faced their past and their future with clear eyes and brave hearts. This book is as much about their journey as it is about Adam's. To the extent that people find reflection, inspiration and lessons about their lives in these pages, it is the Suttons to whom they should offer thanks. Adam knows how lucky he is to have them; Neil is grateful to have been taken into that warm fold.

Heath Ledger's part in this story cannot, of course, be overstated. He was never a more generous and genuine friend to Adam than when he read an all but final draft of this book and got straight on the phone to say simply: 'Bushy, I'm so proud of you.' He didn't want to change a thing. We know him as a man to whom privacy is everything; we cannot thank him enough for being willing to sacrifice a little of that to enable Adam to tell his story more powerfully, and with full support and understanding.

Lastly, thanks to Scout, the dog, who arrived at the start and was still sleeping under the desk when the final word of the epilogue was written. Much like the authors, he didn't know what to do with himself when it was over. And to those trees we kept talking about – hopefully they'll stand forever, reminding us both of what really matters.

Adam and Neil

More great books from
Random House Australia

'My father died thinking that none of us would ever amount to anything worthwhile . . . He had told each of us from a young age that Aboriginal people had bad blood . . . that we were incapable of learning beyond elementary level because Aboriginal people were not as bright as white people.'

Growing up in the 1930s and 40s, Audrey Evans felt like an outsider living between two worlds. Perceived as neither white nor black, at school she was made to sit in the front of the class so that the teachers could look over her, and the only real education she received was in violence, alcoholism and poverty.

In an era when many subjects were taboo, Audrey found herself pregnant at 17 before she was even aware she had lost her virginity. She was barely an adult when she was forced to work as a prostitute and was battling loneliness, depression and the brandy bottle.

Although in the years that followed Audrey faced more than most women could bear in many lifetimes, she stubbornly refused to believe that it was too late to turn her life around. What she did next took more courage than anything she had confronted before. At the same age that most people are thinking of retiring, Audrey applied for a place at university. It was a decision that would change her life – and the lives of those around her – forever.

Many Lifetimes is an extraordinary and ultimately uplifting tale of one woman's triumph over adversity and a powerful reminder that anything is possible.

'A fine book of women, landscapes and the tides of life.'
KATE GRENVILLE
Out of Place
JO DUTTON

Daughter of Italian immigrant Eve, and mother of beautiful Jasmine and headstrong Ella, Nina's life has always been bound to those of other women.

For the girl who longed for freedom and art, her dreams seem distant when she finds herself raising her daughters with only her mother's support. *Out of Place* charts Nina's course through life, from her girlhood, when her mother's European ways are a puzzle and an embarrassment, through her troubled marriage to a man who is always looking elsewhere for happiness, to her struggles as a mother.

But just when these three generations of feisty women seem to be pulling together and looking to a happier future, where their lives and loves can be balanced by distance and independence, a tragic accident tears them apart.

Set against the beaches of Perth and the searing heat and harsh beauty of Central Australia, Jo Dutton delicately illustrates the frustrations, problems, joy and love that each of these generations gives and takes from each other as Nina learns, through heartbreaking lessons, that come what may, her life will always be touched by these three amazing women.

'A fine book of women, landscapes and the tides of life.'
Kate Grenville

'A wonderful read. Ruthlessly honest, passionate, gutsy and funny. I couldn't put it down.'
MAGGIE TABBERER
SALVATION CREEK
An Unexpected Life
SUSAN DUNCAN

'As I bumped across the water in a leaky tin dinghy I didn't know that the journey had begun. That the pale yellow house with a corridor of columns and long verandah on the high, rough hill would hold the key to it all . . .'

At 44 Susan Duncan appeared to have it all. Editor of two of Australia's top-selling women's magazines, a happy marriage to a kindred spirit, a jetsetting lifestyle covering stories from New York to Greenland and rubbing shoulders with Hollywood royalty, she was living large in every way. The world was her oyster.

But when her beloved husband and brother die within three days of each other, her glittering life shatters. In shock, she zips on her work face, climbs back into her high heels and soldiers on – until one morning eighteen months later when she simply can't get out of bed.

Heartbreaking, funny and searingly honest, *Salvation Creek* is the story of a woman who found the courage not only to walk away from a successful career and begin again, but to beat the odds in her own battle for survival and find a new life – and love – in a tiny waterside idyll cut off from the outside world.

'A wonderful read. Ruthlessly honest, passionate, gutsy and funny. I couldn't put it down.' Maggie Tabberer

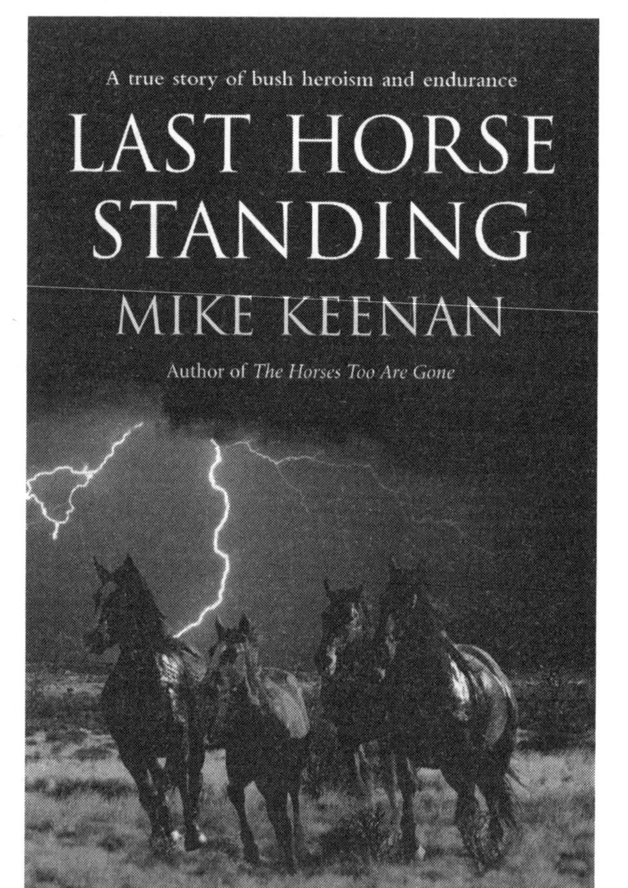
A true story of bush heroism and endurance
LAST HORSE STANDING
MIKE KEENAN
Author of The Horses Too Are Gone

An amazing true story of courage and survival in the outback by the bestselling author of *The Horses Too Are Gone.*

In 1971, bushman Jack Camp went mustering wild cattle – 'cleanskins' – in a vast and isolated stretch of the Kimberley coast. With cattle fetching boom prices, the potential profit would be huge – but so were the risks. It was the unpredictable and dauntingly hot wet season, the region was infested with snakes and crocodiles, and the cattle would have to be swum out across a river notorious for its dramatic tidal surges.

Everything was going according to plan when out of the blue a cyclone struck, flooding the area. The cattle and horses were scattered, the camp and equipment destroyed. Jack, his young son and a teenage stockman were left without food, fire, shelter or a means of escape. No one knew their exact location and they were expected to be gone for some weeks.

As time passed without rescue, Jack decided their only chance was to head for a cattle station some fifty kilometres away. The trouble was, to reach it they would have to cross the shark- and crocodile-infested tidal estuary. With them went the recaptured Bluey, the only survivor after the horses grazed on a poisonous local plant.

And so began a journey that would take them to hell and back. How they made it out is both a gripping yarn and a testament to the determination of the outback spirit. In classic Mike Keenan style, this is an action-packed page-turner that is sure to appeal to fans of his previous books and anyone who is fascinated by tales of bush heroism and endurance.